Sex and Soul Redux

A Memoir of Salvation

Cristina L. White

LETTER
P·E·N
PRESS

Corvallis, Oregon

SEX AND SOUL REDUX
A Memoir of Salvation

Copyright © 2023 by Cristina L. White.

Published by Letter Pen Press, Corvallis, Oregon

All rights reserved. This book may not be reproduced in whole or in part, in any form or by any electronic or mechanical means, without written permission from the author, except by a reviewer, who may quote brief passages in a review. Any member of an educational institution wishing to photocopy part or all of this work for classroom use, or anthology, should contact the author at www.cristinalwhite.com. Thank you for your support of the author's rights.

Edited by Karen Asbelle

Cover and interior design by Ray Rhamey
Published simultaneously in paperback and ebook formats

Library of Congress Control Number: 2023907684
ISBN 978-0-9906261-4-5

Printed in the United States of America

This is a work of nonfiction. Not all—but some—names have been changed in order to protect the privacy of people who had no intention of appearing in an account of the author's life.

For Donna Jayne
All my love, always

Contents

ABOUT THIS REDUX EDITION	1
AN OCEAN OF WOMEN	5
THE RIGHT TO HAPPINESS	7
AN ESTATE OF SIN	25
SALVATION	31
STORIES SHE TELLS ME	36
PERSIMMONS	38
STEPHANIE	42
CAROLYN	48
ZEN MIND, ZEN MUSCLE	57
NEW YORK, DIXIE, NEW YORK	61
THE ROAD TO CARL JUNG COUNTRY	68
TAI CHI AND TRANSITION	77
HEADLINE	83
AWAKENING	88
WHERE IT BEGAN	91
BETWEEN THE JEWELS	94
SARA	96
WHIRLWIND	102
ADVICE	105
NIGHT TALK	107
WORDS	108
WE NEVER MEAN TO FALL IN LOVE	112
SOLSTICE	119
TRESPASS	124
FALL INTO INFINITY	126

SARA'S PRAYER	133
WORKING IT OUT	135
BANSHEE	137
SIX-FIFTHS	140
I AM THE MOST BLESSED OF BEINGS	142
SAVED BY THE NET	146
THE MORAL ARC	148
THE LOVE OF MY LIFE	159
CAROLYN, STEPHANIE, SARA	161
A WEAVE OF WOMEN	165
SURPRISE	187
PEACEFUL	192
EPILOGUE	194
ACKNOWLEDGMENTS	195
Thank You	198
Also By Cristina L. White	199

ABOUT THIS REDUX EDITION

Redux is a Latin word meaning "brought back" or "returned." Though there are other synonyms for redux—such as "refreshed" and "renewed"—the definition that resonates for me is "returned." In *Sex and Soul Redux*, I have returned to a memoir that was begun in 2009 and completed in 2014. Five years were spent writing, rewriting, editing and then proofing the final manuscript. After all that was accomplished, the manuscript went to a talented book designer—he took charge of the interior and exterior design. When the manuscript became a book in 2014, I gave away some copies, enjoyed modest sales, and went on to other work.

Early in 2022, I read my memoir again. I have always been glad I wrote *Sex and Soul*; I still feel that way. But in certain ways, I was unhappy with the book. There were passages I wanted to rewrite, because I could see clearer approaches to the same descriptive material. Near the end of the memoir, there were brief sections that no longer seemed necessary. I had also alluded to a poem that I failed to include, and it felt like a glaring omission.

Another omission that demanded my attention had to do with a relationship that was notable for its extremes at the start and finish—wonderfully positive at the start and then winding its way downward to a miserable end.

The relationship had spurred me to move to Sonoma County in Northern California. That move, along with the attempt to begin anew with someone I greatly admired, marked an important juncture in my life. Yet I concluded that significant time-span with one sentence: "The relationship ended a year and some months later, and I came out of it with my self-confidence deeply shaken." I had written nothing about how I had lost confidence in myself—nothing about the circumstances that led to my bruised ego and broken heart. As a reader returning to this memoir with fresh eyes, I felt much like a good friend of mine who—after reading about that "year and some months"—had asked: what happened? It may be that I had avoided saying more because certain events during the course of the relationship had been so intensely painful.

In retrospect, I felt the need to give some account of what I had experienced, both during the relationship and in its aftermath. Not unlike some others after a break-up, I was emotionally bruised and in need of a way to mend my frayed ego. That need caused me to become a student of psychology, and then to a deeper exploration of the healing arts—a field of study that would lead to a through-line in my work as a writer and a teacher. My endeavor to understand the psyche and the healing process led to a philosophy that came to underpin my entire creative and spiritual life.

It's been nine years since this memoir was first published. The events I originally recorded haven't changed, although—in some ways—I have changed. I wanted *Sex and Soul Redux* to reflect my current perspective.

In considering this redux edition, I turned to writers I admire—masters of this craft where I am still forging my way. I found anecdotal evidence of writers returning to work that had already been published in order to rewrite and revise their work. To mention only three of many examples: John Fowles published *The Magus* in 1966. Twelve years later he published a revised version. Walt Whitman apparently spent his lifetime rewriting *Leaves of Grass*. And there is this quote by Vladimir Nabokov: "*I have often rewritten—often several times—every word I have ever published. My pencils outlast their erasers.*"

Cristina L. White, 2023

AN OCEAN OF WOMEN

If melancholy ruled a season, autumn would be its domain. Even on sunlit days, when the crimson leaves are so bright they seem to singe the air, I sense a trace of gray that dims the brightness. Like a wisp of fog that gathers mass and subdues the landscape, the gray permeates my senses and pervades my thoughts. As I walk along the quiet streets of my neighborhood on this November day, I let myself sink into the melancholy and find its source: I am aware of my own mortality. The brightness of the season foreshadows the darkness of winter, and in the rustle of autumn leaves, I hear nature's annual reminder that we all die. Take stock, she says. Nothing, no one, is forever.

I think it was that reminder that led me to gather these pages torn from another era, an era intensely lived, hastily sketched. I lay the pages out, one by one, and realize I must complete my sketches, and fill in the shadows that edge the light. That task has led me here. I am writing out of instinct, and a need that is both simple and complex. I want to talk about women I have loved, and my struggle against the forces determined to shut me away from that love.

Perhaps the woman I was and the women I have known are beckoning me into the past, calling me back so that I may deepen my understanding of the woman I have become. I heed the call, and submerge myself in memory, in a river of memories, drifting, following the current down to the sea. Down to the sea, and out—into an ocean of women.

THE RIGHT TO HAPPINESS

I grew up in a world where it seemed all women were meant to marry, and it was expected that every girl wanted to be a bride. I wanted to be Roy Rogers. I was a cowboy out to save the day, riding an imaginary stallion across limitless miles of open range. In those daydreams of galloping to the rescue, not once did I imagine myself as a bride, and yet I did a credible imitation of being one at the tender age of nine.

I still have the photograph. I'm wearing a white dress trimmed with lace. It has puffy short sleeves, a demure rounded collar, and a white satin sash at the waist, tied over a generously full skirt. My black hair has been permed for the occasion, and the tight curls are adorned with a small, veiled headband. No one, including me, thought of this ritual attire as a bridal gown or described it as one. But now, as I look at that little girl in her First Communion dress, I realize that this was as close as I ever got to the wedding my mother dreamed of for me.

While the preliminary machinations were not as elaborate as those for a wedding ceremony, there were serious preparations for this major event in my Catholic upbringing. Apart from catechism lessons on the meaning of the sacrament of the Holy Eucharist, there was all the time and thought my mother put into the dress she made for me.

During the '50s, it was a given that many women sewed for themselves and their children. My mother, however, was a professional seamstress. She had owned a dress shop in the Philippines when she was in her twenties. The daughter of a native Filipina and a Navy man from Memphis, Louise had been born and raised in Manila, on the island of Luzon. In the '30s, like other young women in that cosmopolitan tropic city, Louise was caught up in a swirl of frequent parties and nights out on the town. Whether it was at a social gathering or a night club, she always showed up in stylish dresses and gowns. Other women soon found out that she had made, and frequently designed, the dresses they were admiring. They started asking her to sew for them, and Louise proceeded to set up shop.

It was at a party, some years after going into business for herself, that Louise met my father, Ismael, a merchant marine who was called Smiley by his friends. She told me that he was the center of attention when she first walked into the room, because he had taken the microphone and was up on the dais with the band, crooning a popular love song of the day.

My mother's romance with Smiley was brief and their love story ill-fated. Though he had told his whole family about Louise and the child they were expecting, my father was far away when I was born in Manila in November 1941. A month and three days after I came into the world, Japan attacked Pearl Harbor. Ten hours later, the Japanese began their invasion of the Philippines. On December 8th, President Roosevelt signed the declaration of war against Japan, and the distance between my parents was abruptly expanded by World War II.

My mother, on her own with a babe in arms, spent the first part of the war in a Japanese prison camp. She was born with dual citizenship and refused to renounce her U.S. citizenship. That refusal meant imprisonment with American civilians in the Santo Tomas Internment Camp in Manila. The quarters were ramshackle and food was scarce. After two years, along with a number of other prisoners, we were released. With me in tow, she spent the remainder of the war traveling with the Filipino Resistance, helping to undermine the Japanese occupation forces. Meanwhile, my father had become a sergeant in the U.S. Army. He returned to the Pacific near the end of the war, only to be killed during the invasion of Luzon, the island where his story with Louise had begun.

Two years after the war ended, my mother met and married my stepfather, a military officer from Des Moines, Iowa. We began a new life in the United States. A beautiful and vivacious woman, Louise became a full-time housewife and mother. My First Communion dress may have been the most elaborate outfit she had made since those heady pre-war days in Manila.

While my mother was engrossed in the dress she was making for me, I was enthralled with the story I was being told in my catechism classes. It was a story in which I was embarking on an epic journey. My mission was to prepare my body, mind, and soul to receive the Holy Eucharist. All the preparation would culminate in the singular moment when a priest would transform a simple wafer into the sacred body of Jesus Christ and offer it to me. By accepting the Eucharist, I would take Christ into my own body. God and I were going to become one.

In order to be ready for this rite of passage, I had to be pure, without sin or stain or blemish. I had to examine my thoughts, as well as my emotions and actions, and make my First Confession, after which I was given a penance. And like everyone taking communion, I had to fast beforehand. There was no food for me on that morning, and nothing to drink except water. I did everything that was required, filled with a sense of gravity in each step taken toward the moment when I would receive the Holy Eucharist. I had a wholehearted belief in the transformation I was about to undergo.

In addition to the formal photo I posed for that day, I have two black-and-white snapshots of my First Communion Sunday. In one, taken in front of our church in Pittsburg, California, my veiled headband has been replaced with a small straw hat with a round brim. I'm standing with a friend who has also received her First Communion. Our white dresses are hemmed to fall well below the knee, and we are both wearing white ankle socks and buckled shoes. In the other photo, I'm beside a parade float that seems to have materialized for the occasion. There is a huge and handsome white paper maché horse on the float. I don't remember the parade or the float, but given that I was already horse-crazy, I'm sure I asked to have my photograph taken with this majestic fantasy steed.

The truth is, I don't remember anything about that day, except for the moment of communion. That image is in my memory only, yet it is far more vivid than the photos in my family album. I remember kneeling at the altar rail, with the sunlight pouring in through the high arched windows on my right. I remember the priest holding a round, white wafer in front of my upturned face. I opened my mouth, the wafer was placed on my tongue, and I swallowed. And for a few seconds, I experienced what I can only describe as pure ecstasy.

That same wave of feeling coursed through me again at certain times during my adolescence, but never again did I feel that intense connection with God while inside the confines of a church. After that particular Sunday, it was only when I was outdoors that I could feel the same awareness of a mysterious and invisible life force. The heartbeat of God, his breath and his pulse, were present for me only in the sanctity of nature.

Those early experiences of God in nature are deeply impressed in my memory. The images, sounds and emotions are still clear and alive. In contrast, for the first five years after my First Communion, I have no memory of being in church.

Blair, my stepfather, was a Unitarian, and I don't remember him attending Sunday service of any kind. I do remember getting dressed in proper Sunday wear to attend Mass with my mother. And I have vague memories of visiting renowned cathedrals in Rome and Paris while we were living in Germany. But after my First Communion, I have no distinct memory of being in church, or at Mass, until I was fourteen and living in Petersburg, Virginia. That was when I began to have questions about God, and my relationship with religion started to unravel.

I was in the eighth grade. It was the first and only year between grades one and twelve that I attended a Catholic school. My enrollment there may have had a lot to do with proximity. The school was little more than a block away from the house where we were living, and the walk to and from St. Joseph School was along a safe residential street.

Each weekday began on the second floor of St. Joseph's, in a large classroom with many windows. It was my homeroom, and there I studied certain subjects with Mrs. Magruder, a short, sturdy woman with auburn hair. She was a good teacher, and firm with us, but I had no fear of her. All my fear was given over to the afternoon hours, when I had to go down to a first-floor classroom and learn history from Sister Dominic.

Sister Dominic was tall and bony and fierce, with a face like a hawk. And like that fearsome bird, she would swoop down to strike terror into anyone who had not studied or wasn't paying attention. Because of Sister Dominic, more than at any other time during my school years, I was getting a lot of religion along with a good education. And I was beginning to ask questions about what I was learning. I had the courage to challenge Mrs. Magruder on the subject of algebra; it made no sense to me. But I never once dared to question Sister Dominic, although I knew that the God she presented didn't quite tally with the one I spoke to in the privacy of my own prayers.

It was at Mass, on the Sunday before Ash Wednesday—the beginning of Lent—when my unspoken questions and internal arguments reached the point of silent but real defiance. My mother wasn't with me, because she had gone to the airport in Richmond to meet my grandmother, Romana, who was arriving from the Philippines. After years of letters back and forth, Louise had finally persuaded her mother to leave Manila and come to live with us. I was on my own that day, seated near the back of the church with some friends who lived in my neighborhood.

It was a big church with a high ceiling, and the Mass at that mid-morning hour was well attended. I looked past all the people in their Sunday best to the priest, who was far in front at an elevated lectern. He began delivering a sermon about the meaning of Lent, and the importance of sacrifice during those forty days before Easter.

Somehow his sermon led to the subject of movies. He thought it was important for everyone, especially young people, to think about their movie-going habits, and how often they went to the movies. He spoke directly to all the children and adolescents present in church, because he wanted us to make a specific commitment of self-sacrifice. He asked us to stand and repeat a statement he had prepared for us. We were to speak the vow aloud, and make the commitment in our minds and in our hearts.

He wanted us to give up movies for Lent.

No. No. *No.* That was all I could hear inside my head. Everything in me balked. I loved the movies. I loved the people in the movies. And though I hadn't yet dared to dream it out loud, I wanted to be in the movies. That dream began to take form when I went to see my first movie musical. It had thrilled me. I wanted to be part of all that singing and dancing.

My favorite musical was *Singin' in the Rain*. After seeing it, a new me was born. I wanted to be Gene Kelly. Along with everything wonderful about it—the cast, the comedy, the great song-and-dance numbers—*Singin' in the Rain* gave me and my best friend a terrific song to belt out as we splashed along wet sidewalks on rainy autumn afternoons.

Movies made me happy.

Now I was being told to stand and swear to give up movies. All my instincts were to stay seated and keep my mouth shut. Why did it matter so much? What would it cost me to forego, for the next several weeks, a handful of movie tickets that were my passport to happiness?

At the time, I couldn't have articulated my reasons. The thought of it had the same effect on me as the algebraic formulas that left me stymied. I could not, for the life of me, grasp why x should equal y. Who says it equals y? And why does it equal y? Like those constructs that left me stranded in a mathematical wilderness, giving up movies was incomprehensible. In modern terms, it did not compute. Now, when I look back on those years spent with my mother and stepfather, I understand that every interest of mine—every affection and passion, every throughline to happiness—was a lifeline.

I lived in a home where happiness was fragile and inconstant. Though we were seldom happy, I believe that our small family unit wanted happiness. I remember the sense of relief when certain events that might have led to discord turned out to be funny instead. The most notable one was a picnic that went awry.

After traveling several miles to a beautiful park with a lake and well-tended grounds, my parents and I discovered we had forgotten our picnic basket. We were surrounded by acres of lawn and trees, and there were no food stalls or vendors of any kind in the park. It was Sunday, and everything was closed in the nearest town. All we had with us was some fruit in a paper bag. We laughed and made the best of it, and ended up having a lovely time. I felt as if an angel had swept a golden cloud of harmony over us. The afternoon could have so easily become one of accusation and blame.

Happiness was a treasure, and I knew its value. On those rare occasions when I made a genuine connection with my stepfather, or when my parents were getting along and the three of us were enjoying each other's company, I wanted to believe that happiness would last, but it never did. Those islands of peace seemed produced by a magician's sleight of hand. The curtain inevitably fell, returning us to a reality of strife and conflict.

My memories of happiness are distinct. I never took that sense of elation for granted. I knew that I was almost always happy spending time with my mother—planting a garden, dancing to records or the radio, listening to her stories. That happiness expanded when my grandmother settled in with us.

Romana had a fine sense of humor and she brought, at least for a while, some balance and leavening to the intensity in our home. I remember watching television with her and both of us laughing as she repeated particular words in an effort to improve her English. After she heard Tennessee Ernie Ford say "Texas," she repeated it—firmly and with conviction: "Taxes." The state of Taxes seemed wonderfully funny to me. I broke out laughing and Romana laughed because I was laughing. Then I tried to explain the difference between Texas and taxes. More laughter.

One day, when it was just my mother, my grandmother and me at home, my mother was attempting to make light of the discord in her marriage. I still remember, and love, my grandmother's response—it was a cogent summary of life in our household.

"Arguments," claimed my mother, "are the spice of life."

"Too much *es*-spice," Romana said.

Happiness was a gift I unwrapped whenever I curled up with a book. I also found it in time spent with friends. In the community theatre groups I became a part of, happiness was in the fun of camaraderie, and in the joy of creativity when bringing plays to life. It was in the peace and solace and wonder I found in the experience of nature. And happiness was certainly mine in a darkened movie house, where I could immerse myself in the tales told on the great silver screen.

Those were stories where happy endings were possible, and they were a perfect antidote for what ailed me at home. I was a girl laboring to maintain a civil attitude toward my stepfather, struggling against overwhelming hatred for this man who was causing so much misery in our household.

I can see now what was good in Blair. I can see the ways in which he tried to be a decent father. But there was too much in him that his own father had thwarted; it made him cold, and alcohol made him abusive. That behavior wasn't consistent or constant, but it was behavior that cut deep, and it happened often enough to leave permanent scars. The deepest cut was made on a bitter cold Christmas Eve, when we were stationed in Munich, Germany.

My memory of that night in Munich begins in a tavern, where I'm seated at a table with my parents and a family friend, a man whose nickname is Ace. My stepfather is an officer; Ace is his sergeant. I'm vaguely aware that Ace works with my stepfather and that Blair is his superior. They get along well, and since Ace is a single man who is far away from his family in the States, he's been invited to spend the evening with us.

My mother likes to go to Midnight Mass on Christmas Eve. I'm old enough now to stay up late and go with her. Blair loves German beer; he's brought us to this tavern before taking my mother and me to Mass. The tavern is crowded; everyone is drinking. The voices around me are loud and the atmosphere is boisterous.

I stay quiet, listening to the talk of the grown-ups. My parents are sitting next to each other, across the table from me and Ace. Blair has a stein of beer in front of him, one of several he's already consumed. At some point, he makes a remark that leads me to ask a question. I don't remember his remark or my question. I only remember his answer.

He's drunk, and his voice is surly when he looks at me and says, "Because hers is bigger than yours."

I don't understand what he's saying, but I do know that it has something to do with sex. My mother is furious, and tells him not to talk to me like that. Blair turns on her, matching her anger with his own. I go blank. I don't know what they're saying. All I know is that they're fighting again. It's as if I'm watching my parents arguing in a silent film. Then the film cuts abruptly to another scene.

I'm standing in the doorway of the tavern, looking out across a parking lot. At the far end of the lot, I can see Blair and my mother, facing one another. I know they're still arguing, but I can't hear them. Blair is six feet tall and well over two hundred pounds. He towers over my mother. I'm not meant to see what happens next, what Blair is doing, and my vision is blurred, or perhaps protected, by the snowfall.

There is another abrupt scene change in the film, and now the audio track is turned on. I'm in the passenger seat of the car. My stepfather is driving, and I'm listening to my mother's muffled sobs in the back seat as we drive home. Ace is sitting next to her, awkwardly trying to comfort her.

Instead of going to Midnight Mass, we return home.

Sometime during the night, I awake and hear water running. I get up and follow the sound, walking slowly, quietly, down the hallway. I see my mother standing at the bathroom sink, washing away the blood that is still flowing from her swollen face. She looks at me and says, "Go back to bed, Cristina." Her tone is deadly calm; her voice comes from a distance I cannot fathom.

And then it is morning, and I'm sitting beside the Christmas tree with my mother and Blair. We are a miserable, nearly silent trio. My parents sit in separate chairs on either side of the tree. I sit between them on the floor, distributing presents, going through the motions of gift-giving. There is the rustle of tissue paper and the whisper of ribbons. No one really talks, but

Blair tries to express the right sentiments; I also try. My mother says nothing.

Blair hands me the present he has chosen for me, a new doll. The only doll I have is one my mother gave me when I was six years old; I brought her with me from the Philippines. Her name is Alice and I love her. She is a baby that I can rock in my arms. She has a little cap with a silk ribbon and her dress is long, made of a soft, light-blue fabric.

The doll Blair has chosen for me is big and stiff, with blue eyes and glossy, red-brown hair. She wears a peach-colored dress trimmed with lace; it shows off her long legs. I thank Blair, politely. I do not say "I hate her." I don't understand why I hate her; I only know that I do. She stays in her gift box, a kind of coffin where my mind relegates Christmas for as long as I live in my stepfather's house.

Right after that dismal scene by the Christmas tree, my mother and I both got dressed and left the house. She took me to the home of a friend, where I stayed curled in the window seat of an alcove, reading a book. I don't recall other children being there, though they may have been in some other part of the house. I'm unsure now if my mother was in another room talking with her friend about what to do next, or if she actually went somewhere else. All I remember is my book and my solitary place next to a window. I was safe there, and warm, deeply absorbed in a Nancy Drew mystery. I read it—from beginning to end—in one sitting. I still credit the author, Carolyn Keene, for saving my mind that Christmas Day.

I don't know now if it was at the end of that day, or the next day, but my mother and I did go back to Blair. She returned to her marriage and I returned with her to the only family unit I knew. By the time New Year's Eve arrived, our life together had resumed some semblance of normalcy. At least, I wanted to believe that it had—I'm not sure how long it took for my mother to recover, physically or emotionally. When I look back on that period, I'm certain there was little my mother could do besides return to her husband. We were in a foreign country, an ocean away from any sort of financial independence she might have been able to secure in the States.

Early in her marriage to Blair, when I was very young, my mother had sometimes gathered me up in the night so we could run away. In Munich, I had seen what we were running from, but that Christmas Eve experience was so traumatic that I hadn't been able to take it all in; my system had gone into shock.

That shock took the form of a specific amnesia—to this day, I have no recollection of Christmas between the ages of twelve and twenty-one, neither the day nor the season. I can remember other seasons, events, and experiences during those years. But having seen more than I could bear in Munich, I believe my psyche erected a barrier to protect me from Christmas Eve and Christmas Day. It was only later, when I was living on my own, that I began to be aware of Christmas and to experience it again. And even then, it was several more years before

I realized that—for a decade of my life—any memory of December 24th and 25th was entirely blocked out.

By the time I was a teenager, in Petersburg, Virginia, I understood the intermittent, middle-of-the-night escapes that had occurred during my childhood, because adolescence brought more of the same. After our three-year tour in Germany, when we had returned to the States, we left my stepfather again. This time, though I hadn't witnessed Blair hitting my mother, I saw her injuries, and I felt no confusion about what had happened. I had seen her with similar injuries in Munich, but at fourteen I was old enough to absorb the shock, and I was deeply relieved when I thought my mother had decided to quit Blair for good.

We fled to Asbury Park in New Jersey and stayed there with friends. For a brief period of time, less than a month, my mother and I were able to live without the threat of Blair's abuse looming over us. Though my mother was a skilled seamstress, resourceful and intelligent, she must still have been scrabbling during that time to figure out how we were going to live on our own. But I had no awareness of that. My life during those days and weeks was akin to being in heaven. I was enrolled in a new school, and I loved my homeroom teacher. He was a man who I would later understand was a progressive—in the mid-1950s, when the general assessment of women was that they were neither smart enough nor able enough for most professions, my teacher made no distinction between boys and girls in their abilities. He set no limits on what girls could learn and achieve. A brand-new world opened up for me. Everything seemed possible. But then Blair showed up at the door, and he begged my mother to come home, begged her to return with him to Virginia.

I don't know how many hours or days it took him to convince her that it would all be different from then on, or what the negotiations entailed. He may have agreed to help with all the paperwork and cost involved in bringing my grandmother to the States to live with us. Whatever he told my mother, whatever he promised—in the end—she agreed to go back to him.

I didn't understand her decision. For myself and even more for my mother, I desperately wanted a life that didn't include my stepfather. Though my frequent and heartfelt prayer had once been to ask God to please, please, let my parents stop fighting, my prayer now was for their marriage to end. But each time she left Blair, my mother's friends persuaded her to return, as did his pleas for forgiveness. I had to live with her decision, just as she did, and make the best of it.

Having all that to contend with, I knew at some visceral level that happiness—and whatever brought me happiness—was deeply and profoundly important. I wasn't about to let go of any part of it.

When the priest in that Petersburg church decided it would be appropriate for us to deny ourselves moviegoing during Lent, he made an arbitrary determination about what was good for us. I saw no good in giving up movies. I was willing to make a sacrifice for Lent, but unwilling to make that particular sacrifice. I believe now that I was obeying a primordial instinct for self-preservation, though in that moment, I only knew that *this* was not a sacrifice God would ask of me. I knew God and I loved God, and I felt God knew and loved me. I did not know the priest. He might say he loved me, as he loved everyone in the congregation, but that was an abstraction. God's love was real.

It seemed clear that the priest, like Sister Dominic, didn't understand God in the same way I did. And now, my understanding was in conflict with the commitment I was being told to make.

As all the young people were asked to stand up, I hesitated. Then, as my friends stood to join everyone else, I rose to my feet. I listened as the priest recited, slowly, the solemn vow that we were to repeat after him. I stood quite still, silent and strangely aware of this critical moment in my life. With no forewarning, I had come to a crossroads, and there was no turning back.

I did not take the vow to give up movies—not in words, nor in thought. On that Sunday, at the age of fourteen, I took my first stand against the authority of the Roman Catholic Church. I had found a right I needed to defend—one that our Founding Fathers purposely wrote into our Declaration of Independence. Before God, in my mind and in my heart, I proclaimed my right to the pursuit of happiness.

AN ESTATE OF SIN

I remember a quote from a 2010 *Time* magazine article: "Predictions are always dicey, especially about the future." Given a chance to size up the future of a girl who first wanted to be Roy Rogers, and then Gene Kelly, it's my bet that almost anyone in our modern era would say that my real argument with the Catholic Church was not about movies, but about sex and sexual identity. They might conclude that a day would come when religion and I would call it quits, and that God and I, who had become one in the rite of First Communion, were destined for divorce. And I would have to say, yes. And no.

It's true that my argument with Catholicism would evolve from movies to love and sex. It would crystallize in my need to choose who I love according to the dictates of my heart. But in 1955, when I first rebelled against the authority of the Church, sex and sexual identity did not loom large in my mind. I barely understood sex, and I hadn't a clue about sexual identity. I was a tomboy, and no one seemed to worry about it, least of all me. Being attracted to a woman was a concept I didn't "get" until I was in college, and by then there were distinct divisions between me and the Church on several fronts.

In my struggle to become myself, and to hold on to an affinity with the Divine, I was David against Goliath, and I waged a nearly constant battle with the Church. At the same time, I was up against an institution that I couldn't even conceptualize until I was an adult: organized religion. And religion—with constant endorsements from society— had the upper hand for the first two decades of my life.

The spiritual angst that my struggle brought on was nearly always present, and it kept me fenced in and conflicted through most of my adolescence. Breaking free of that agony was a process of untying knots, and eventually opening a door that led out of a dim room where Christ suffered on the cross and the confessional was the central focal point.

In all those years of going to confession, there was only one young priest who—very gently—told me that I was being too hard on myself. The others all seemed to be high priests of purity, absolving the stained, sinful beings who were on their knees before God. I look back and remember times when I stood in line waiting to go into the confessional, wondering what I would say. I couldn't find any real sins; it was all trivia. But that changed over time. Mother Church taught me how to evoke the demon: Linger over your appetites and condemn them; search for your weaknesses and deepen the shadows that surround them.

How obscene it feels now, all those adult minds handing down their darkness to me. Here is your inheritance, Cristina: An estate of sin.

How I longed for purity. Only my passion was pure. Sprawled in an April field, gazing up at the wide blue skies, I was full of love for the earth, full of love for God. God was my beloved, and my beloved was the forsythia, and the deep green scent of crushed leaves. I felt him in the heavy warmth of summer. God was in the sunlight on the glittering silver olive branch. Standing quietly at day's end, wrapped in the color of wisteria at twilight, I rested in his embrace.

My private relationship with God was simple, and perfect. Then, on Sunday mornings in church, that simplicity slipped away. When Mass began, my mind would blur; I lost my bearings. Flickering candles, Christ hanging on the cross, blood on his brow and his hands, blood seeping from his rib cage. A congregation of bodies crowded together, performing in unison the required motions of the service: kneel, sit, stand, kneel. My breathing would grow shallow, and finally I felt as if I could not breathe at all. There was a buzzing in my ears, and a blackness descending all around me. I felt the perspiration on my skin, felt my knees grow weak. Just before fainting, before losing consciousness, I would rush outside where I could breathe. This went on for years. I didn't understand it, and no one seemed able to articulate a cause.

I remember a Sunday when I was sitting on the steps outside the church, trying to clear my head. My mother was standing nearby, watching to see if the dizziness would pass. A stranger was speaking to her, trying to reassure her, telling her that the air inside the church was too heavy on this warm day. Only years later, looking back, did I realize that it wasn't just the air. It was my religion, the Church, the catechism of venial and mortal sins. All of it was too heavy, too stifling and dark.

The God I knew and understood was an invisible presence, made visible in all those places that made my soul sing. He was in the meadow grass, the fragrance of lilacs, the trail of moonlight on the lake. I couldn't reconcile this mysterious and exquisite pulse of life—God as love and beloved— with the wounded man hanging on the cross.

It took me a long time to sort it out, perhaps because I was in a philosophical maze and kept stumbling backward at the only exit the Church provided. Through all my years of questioning, I kept returning again and again to the same question: How was it possible that my feelings of pleasure, joy, the sweet sensation in my body when I first began to fall in love, how could it all be sin? The idea that God would condemn me for being fully alive, or turn against me for feelings that were loving and good, made no sense. Had I known how to argue the point with a priest, I'm certain he would have said that God would never turn against me—it was the sinner who had turned her back on God. But that only led me back to the original question: Were these feelings I was experiencing truly sinful? How could they be, when I still loved God, still felt that God loved me?

Finally, it came down to this: I would not let religion get in the way of my relationship with God. That was my line in the sand. It is where I took a stand all those years ago when the Church tried to erect a barrier of sins between me and God. And that is where I stand today.

When I reflect on the distinction I made between Church and God, I realize it was my mother who first enabled me to make that distinction. She was the quintessential independent. As with everything else in her life, she had her own brand of Catholicism, and being Catholic was secondary to being a believer. She believed in God, and so it followed that God believed in her. God would not condemn her or banish her from his love. She never talked about sin. She never talked about hell. She had gone through a war and near–starvation in a Japanese prison camp, and she had kept herself and her baby alive through all of it. She knew what real hell was.

I didn't discuss religion with my mother. But I could see that, for her, religion was simply a structure that provided a way to practice what she believed at her core. The essence of that core was her faith, and I understood that her faith was based on a very personal relationship with God. The rites of her Catholic religion were important to her, but they were not the main event. The doctrine of her religion informed and guided her choices; it did not dictate them.

Like my mother, I believed in God, and I held fast to my firm conviction in the goodness and loving nature of a Divine force and presence. It was this unwavering conviction that compelled me to question the Church's teachings. That same conviction finally drove me to rebel against the attempt to instill shame in me for feelings that seemed natural and good. My desires were as involuntary as my breathing. While the Church sought to isolate and banish me because of those desires, my spirit connected me to God. Even after my sins had been delineated and punishment threatened, I felt the strength of that connection. After all the internal wrestling with the idea of being "good," and what it meant to love God, my faith remained; it was there, burning bright—a small, steady flame in the dark.

SALVATION

If the primary mission of religion is the salvation of souls, then my primary mission as a young Catholic adult was to understand exactly what the Church meant by salvation. When I left home to go to college at the end of summer, 1960, I encountered a whole new world of ideas and experiences. They led me to question what it meant to be saved, though I didn't think of it in those terms. I only knew I was struggling with feelings and desires that the Church deemed wrong, sinful. At age fourteen, I had been unable to accept a priest's dictum that giving up movies for Lent would be good for me. Now, I began to wonder if religion and I disagreed about the meaning of sin and salvation.

Living on my own gave me a different sense of who I was and what I wanted, and I became increasingly aware of what I can only describe as my "inner body." My spiritual muscle, the canon of my bones, told me that I could no longer fit into the Catholic uniform. That was difficult to accept. Even as I tried to understand the interior upheaval in my religious identity, I could hear religion pounding and hammering at the door. And I knew, if I decided to continue my journey as a Catholic, it would mean I must abide by a very specific Book of Rules. Those rules would dictate a certain course for my life. It was not the course that my emotions, my body, my deepest intuition were guiding me toward.

I had my clearest experience of the growing division between me and the Church when I was nineteen. It was then that I entered the crucible of what was, for me, the ultimate taboo for a good Catholic girl: I fell in love with a woman. She was a talented actress who had what amounted to star status in the Drama Department. We were both cast in a play in which she played the lead and I had a walk-on with one line. Although she was a senior and a star, and I was a new kid on the block, she was generous and welcoming. Refined and reserved by nature, she was also kind. The following semester, she graduated and left San Francisco to pursue a career on the stage. She never knew I felt anything more than friendship for her, as I could barely acknowledge those feelings in myself.

I have a distinct memory of sitting outside on the wide stone steps of the library one cloudy spring day, watching the drift of people on campus, when she came into view. She was off in her own world, perhaps dreaming of her future, or immersed in a new character she was developing in her mind. Content simply to be on the same planet, in a place where there was the possibility of seeing her walk by, I suddenly knew what I felt for her was not simple friendship. This was love, and moreover, it was love that the Church wanted me to suppress and turn away from. According to Religion's Rule Book, my feelings for her would inevitably lead me on the path to perdition. All the happiness I experienced when I saw her, spoke to her—I had to deny all of it. My religion required me to sever emotions that felt as if they were coming from the deep center of my being.

It seemed that religion was a mighty locomotive bearing down on me, while I was bound and knotted to the track. I realized, perhaps just in time, that it was my truest self who was in peril.

Coming to terms with the idea that religion might harm rather than help me was a significant turning point. It was then that my argument with religion, begun in adolescence, was resolved: I understood that my argument was with the Church, not with God. There were two beings who gave me unconditional love. One was visible, the other invisible. Both provided a profound and constant lifeline. My mother loved me. God loved me. Of these two I was certain. In the end, this certainty I felt at my core, the knowledge that I was loved, saved me.

Of course, it took more than that knowledge to break free of religion's hold on me—a few key people opened new doors and changed my perception of the world. My sociology professor was one of them. A thin, soft-spoken man, he shattered an ideology I had never before questioned: the dogma of Catholicism as the one and only universal religion. Over the course of a few months, my acceptance of this tenet disintegrated. That was the ultimate effect of the classes he taught, though I don't think he ever mentioned Catholicism. He simply told us about other societies, other cultures, other ways of living and believing. To my mind, it didn't seem possible that all those other societies, having functioned so well over time with their alternate belief systems, could be entirely wrong. This new perspective began to validate the alternate belief system that was slowly germinating in me.

While it was my sociology professor who changed my view of the Church and the world, it was a therapist who played a critical role in changing the way I saw myself. During those college years, I only went to a counselor once, and I'll never forget him. A heavy-set, big-boned man with a thick moustache and dark brown hair, he came from the Carl Rogers school of therapy. Rogerians believe in letting the patient take the lead. The idea was that the therapist endeavored to remain neutral, thus providing for the patient a kind of blank sheet where one could work out for oneself an answer to life's personal dilemmas. When I told him I had been raised a Catholic, and then confessed my innermost desires—I was in a play, and had a crush on the leading lady—he inadvertently sighed. The sigh was almost inaudible. I heard in that soft sound a world of sympathy for the turmoil I was going through, and in his response, I felt pure acceptance. I knew it was okay with him that I was attracted to a woman, and he understood why I felt conflicted about it. That was okay too. His gentle acceptance helped put me on a path toward my own self-acceptance.

During those early adult years, certain friends were also instrumental in freeing me to open up to a new self-image. They were the trusted few who offered their friendship and never judged me, even when I revealed thoughts and feelings that were, according to the Church, strictly taboo. The first friend I spoke to about my crush on the leading lady was neither shocked nor repelled. I remember the great sense of relief I felt when I found I could share this secret and not lose her friendship. It was she, in fact, who urged me to go to the counseling center. She clearly thought it was time I stopped berating myself for being myself.

And through all my confusion, exploration, and bewildered questioning, there were the women I loved who also loved me. Even when we hurt each other, and fumbled and stumbled our way through relationships, learning how to be together and how to be apart, we were bent on loving, on understanding ourselves and each other, each one of us intent on being true to ourselves.

The women I have loved were central to my salvation, and this is my hymn to them.

STORIES SHE TELLS ME

October 1974. Sunday morning. Stephanie and I are on a rutted country road in Sebastopol, on the western edge of Sonoma County. We drive past fields where cows are grazing and weathered chicken coops sink slowly into the earth behind big farm houses. As we pass an old barn and a long line of eucalyptus trees, Stephanie launches into a tale about last night, spent in the city.

"I got a little crazy," she tells me. Her adventure began at Peg's, a bar in the Richmond District of San Francisco, where Stephanie had thought to while away an hour or two in a familiar hangout. But when she walked in, she spotted a woman who was blonde, gorgeous, and supremely self-confident. "She was racking billiard balls," Stephanie says. "I watched her play pool, and that was it for me."

Stephanie decided she had to know her, and ended up following the woman around in her car for half the night. An evening meant to be spent in the easy camaraderie of other women culminated in a mad chase through the Saturday night streets.

I'm not jealous. At least that's what I tell myself. It's just a playful Stephanie adventure, a way she has of passing the time and keeping herself entertained. I listen to her, exhausted, wishing I could go back to bed. Not enough sleep. Too much emotional juggling. Too many emotions, period. I see a persimmon tree ripe with orange fruit and suddenly, in my mind, I'm back in Manhattan.

PERSIMMONS

It's bright, and cold. Outside, white clouds are scattered across a blue sky. I'm in Julia's tiny Greenwich Village apartment, having coffee with her, when she asks if I want a persimmon. "I've never had a persimmon," I tell her.

"Never had a persimmon?" She smiles. "Let me get you one."

I've known Julia since my student days in San Francisco. She grew up on a ranch in New Mexico. Through her entire childhood, she never ate a candy bar, never drank a Coke, never had a cavity. She's proud of that record, and still refuses soda and candy. Julia has long copper hair, blue eyes, and a slender, boyish body. She's wearing today what she almost always wears—jeans, a white cotton shirt, and a buff-colored suede jacket. On her feet, moccasins. I love Julia's intelligence and talent. There's a restlessness about her that makes me think of untamed ponies in green country pastures, and the feel of a fresh morning breeze on your face. She's attractive and confident and seems always to have a lover.

Once, more than a little drunk, I was standing close to Julia in a crowded San Francisco bar. I asked her, in an indirect way, if she slept with women. I'm sober as I write this, and I can't figure out how to ask that question without being direct. Maybe the alcohol helped me to blur the question, but it certainly didn't blur her answer. She said no. I was disappointed, but that was that.

Now we're both living in Manhattan, storming the walls of the New York theatre world, hoping to make something of ourselves. Thanks to Julia, I have turned on to grass and hash. I get stoned as often as possible, because I love being high. I'm still attracted to Julia, but I have no illusions about being with her. I content myself with enjoying her friendship and her always interesting lovers.

The current one is a young poet who recently traveled south of the border, where he had the misfortune of being arrested. He managed to escape from a Mexican jail, and it makes for a harrowing story. He is tall, handsome, with jet black hair and liquid brown eyes. To the romantic in me, which is pretty much all of me, he looks like a living, breathing, artist's rendering of the idealized poet.

The poet left us barely half an hour ago, and I wait quietly on my own in a sparsely furnished living room. Julia returns from the kitchen with a persimmon, a deep-blue ceramic plate, and a paring knife. She sets the plate before me on a low table, then places the small knife and the orange persimmon on the plate. "The texture is a little unusual," she says. "That's what puts most people off. And they have to be ripe, or else they leave a fuzz on your teeth that'll drive you insane. They have to be just right."

Gently, carefully, she splits the fruit open with the knife and quarters it. I observe as she eats one quarter, bending the skin back and watching the rich fruit burst open. I can see that Julia loves the sensuousness of it. I copy her, bringing a slice up to my lips and letting my mouth slide over the soft fibrous tissue, then biting in. Delicious. Caught in a sudden rush of images, I find I'm smiling. I realize that Julia, with her interesting lovers and wildly free sexual ways, has never traveled the territory I have explored with women. The sweet, soft persimmon flesh evokes memories of my most intimate moments with the women I have loved. As the taste of the fruit lingers on my tongue, those memories course through me, and I'm glad. Glad of my experience in loving and being loved by a woman, and the places we have traveled together.

Nine years later, I'm driving through the California countryside on my way to cook brunch for a friend. Beside me is Stephanie, who is seven years younger than I am. Sensing that her story of the beautiful blonde pool player has sent me away to my own thoughts, Stephanie engages me in talk of food, specifically, the food we're going to prepare for brunch. Women and food, good wine and good coffee, these are Stephanie's favorite subjects. She is fair, pretty, with long brown hair that is silky and fine. There's an openness to her face, a kind of innocence. She's light-hearted, easy-going, generous.

I'm happy with Stephanie. I feel married to her, married in a way my parents would never understand—not only because we're two women together, but also because we've formalized our liaison with a contract. Stephanie proposed this arrangement, and I agreed. The contract is this: once a year, we review where we are, what we want and don't want, and what we need. Then we decide whether to go on, and how to go on. Nothing is forever, says Stephanie, and she cannot promise how she'll feel tomorrow. Making no promises, we've been together for two years. This year, Stephanie wanted the freedom to explore other relationships. On the edge of dissolving our union, we decided to live apart, and that has led us to fall in love again.

STEPHANIE

Stephanie came into my life because of my friendship with Ann, a single mother with two children. Ann kept food on the table and a roof overhead by working as an administrative director for a graduate program at Sonoma State, a job that often required her to juggle her time and commitments. More than anyone else, it was Ann who had persuaded me to apply for the Master's Program in Humanistic Psychology at the college. In February of 1972, I was several months into the work required to earn my M.A. degree, and I remember walking with Ann across campus one day, getting in a short visit before we each went on to our separate schedules.

She told me that a young woman named Stephanie had moved into a corner bedroom of the old house she owned in Cotati, not far from the college campus. Stephanie had recently returned from a trip to Europe, and had used her savings to get there and back. She had spent her time walking and hitching rides across several countries, soaking in the cultures of the continent. Now, to offset the rent, she was making herself available to help Ann with her children, staying with them and helping out as needed whenever Ann couldn't be there. Considering the demands of Ann's job, Stephanie was a godsend. Ann trusted her and the kids loved her, so the new arrangement was working well.

Not long after that walk with Ann, I found myself one March afternoon with a break between seminars. I drove away from campus under a clouded sky, with the car window open to the mild air. I knew it was a day that Ann was normally off, and I decided to stop by her house. She was in the kitchen, slightly exasperated because she had just had a phone call from a co-worker informing her of some emergency at the college that required her attention. That meant she couldn't drive her son and daughter to an event later in the day, as she had planned to do.

"Now I have to figure out how to get them there," she said.

"Is Stephanie here?" I hadn't even met Stephanie, but Ann's description of her had given me the impression that she was someone who could be relied on in situations like this. "Can she take them?"

"She doesn't have a car."

"What about your car?"

"Then how do I get to my office?"

"I can take you. I have to go back anyway."

Ann considered this for a moment. Apparently, when Ann had talked with Stephanie about taking care of the kids, it had been about her staying at home with them. The possibility of driving Ann's car hadn't been discussed.

"Hey, Stephanie," Ann called.

I watched Stephanie saunter toward us along the hallway. My first impression of her was of the girl next door in the body of a young earth mother. Big-breasted, big-boned, with a beautiful complexion, Stephanie exuded health. She was wearing jeans, a tank top, and gold hoop earrings.

"Yes?"

"Do you think you can drive my station wagon?" Ann asked her.

"Is it any different from driving a Mack truck?"

Ann and I both burst out laughing. I liked Stephanie instantly. There in Ann's kitchen, in that outburst of laughter, Stephanie and I began our friendship.

A few months later, in October, I became Stephanie's lover. Soon after that, Stephanie got her own car, an old Rambler, and she decided to move to new digs. It was a separate structure, a room built to one side of a house in the hills above Cotati. The room measured six by eight feet and nearly all the floor space was given over to a big bed, where we spent many pleasurable hours together. There were windows that looked out on oak trees and a winding country road edged with wild grass and Queen Anne's lace. Across the road was a weathered fence and pastureland that sloped up to the sky.

Sometimes, when the weather was fine, Stephanie would get her fiddle out and stand beneath the trees outside the house. She would lift the fiddle to her shoulder and begin to play, sending music out along the road and up into the hills. I would sit by the open window, watching her and listening, swept away by her skill and the joy in her music.

November 1974. Stephanie is living at the southern end of Cotati, in a small place she has built herself out of rummaged wood. The lane leading to it is unpaved; the nearest house is some distance away, adjacent to the narrow rural road that goes into town.

On a Thursday, near midnight, I arrive at Stephanie's cottage. The rain has stopped and the sky is a deep blue-black with pinpoints of starlight. Stray white clouds drift by, lit by a moon that is still bright, but waning. I'm high. I step into the darkness of Stephanie's yard and see a kerosene lamp and the glow of candlelight in the windows of her home. They lend a soft radiance to the colors of the crazy-quilt curtains.

Stephanie is expecting me, but she is probably asleep at this hour. She is early to bed, early to rise. I open the door quietly and see everything I was drawn to when I first met Stephanie on that cloudy, early spring day two years ago.

Her love of the rustic country life is all here, in this cottage of patchwork natural wood. Mason jars filled with grains, beans, and loose-leaf teas line the weather-beaten shelves of her kitchen. There are ceramic cups and bowls, wooden spoons, antique kitchenware. My tapestry rug is on the wall beside her bed; nearby is a child-size oak desk. To one side of the room there is a round table with straw flowers at the center and a low, heavy bowl of scented candles.

I am charmed by her space, charmed by who she is. I love this place filled with plants, picture rocks, seashells. I love her fine voice and good guitar, love that she is both cook and carpenter. She can swing a hammer, maneuver a power saw, and fix your car. But when she invites a lady for lunch there is a carafe of good wine on the table, rich cheese, fresh parsley from the garden, and soup she has made herself. And it is all wonderful.

The other morning, drinking coffee, I thought of Stephanie, of her insistence that coffee be fresh, rich, flavorful. I once told a friend that Stephanie had won me with good coffee. It was the autumn when we became lovers, when she was living in that separate room where her bed occupied most of the space. On one wall was a shelf of blue mason jars, all of them filled with coffee beans: French roast, Arabian, Columbian, Ethiopian. Nearby, in its own place, was a beautiful antique coffee grinder. Each morning, Stephanie would ask what kind of coffee I wanted. While I was still waking up, she would grind the beans by hand in the antique grinder, then disappear into the kitchen. A short while later she would return with two cups and hand me one of them. Our mornings began with an incredibly delicious brew and a dark coffee aroma filling the room. That was when I became addicted to good coffee—and to Stephanie.

CAROLYN

Thanksgiving Day, 1974. The sky over San Francisco is clear and the sun is warm. Stephanie and I drive out to the ocean and pull in at the wide driveway that leads into a rough level lot on a hillside above Seal Rock. We look out at the remains of the Sutro Baths—a once wonderful place that can only be remembered now, in old tinted postcards and black-and-white photographs of another era. The baths themselves have been reduced to lines of jagged concrete eternally washed by the ocean, their broken stone fragments patrolled by seagulls.

The sea is a deep cobalt blue, calm, incredibly beautiful, sparkling in the sunlight. We walk along the curve of Geary Boulevard to the Cliff House and stop there to have an Irish coffee. We indulge our senses in the earthy, spirited scent of whiskey and the smoothness of the thick cream. Sitting by a window where we can look out at the ocean, we admire the view and each other, appreciating how good we look in our holiday clothes, how good we look together.

Stephanie has to work, so I drop her off at the catering company job that enables her to pay the rent. Then I drive to North Beach and park my car under the trees in front of the Art Institute. North Beach is quiet. I walk to Saints Peter and Paul Church across from Washington Square Park, and go inside to say a long thank-you to God and my friend Saint Anthony. On this day given to gratitude, I offer thanks for a contract I've signed, and for a small advance that has given me time to finalize a manuscript before delivering it to a local publishing house that is solid, reputable.

I head up to Coit Tower. There, on the upper edge of the boulevard that ascends Telegraph Hill, I pause in front of a persimmon tree stripped bare by winter of all its leaves. Near the top, forming a close, friendly circle, there are three ripe persimmons. At the very top is one tiny persimmon, all alone.

I look east to an orange-gray haze above the hills of Berkeley and Oakland. The waters of the San Francisco Bay are a perfect backdrop for the persimmon tree. On the water, there's a freighter and three sailboats. With my hands, I form a narrow enclosure to frame the cluster of persimmons. I imagine them as they might appear in a Japanese painting. Then a tugboat chugs into view and pulls me back into the scene before me. I relax my arms and contemplate the stretch of city on the hillside below. I feel peaceful. I'm grateful to be myself. Grateful that I'm not Carolyn.

I first met Carolyn in Manhattan, when a friend took me to a Chelsea theatre to see a play. Near the end of it, a young woman dressed in a long, green velvet dress stepped out to one side of the stage. She was fair and blonde, with fine hair that fell to her shoulders. I remember nothing about the play, only her, all alone in a pool of light, singing an old English ballad in a high, clear voice. We were introduced backstage. Along with a few other people, I was invited to a party at her place, a small ground floor apartment near Tompkins Square Park in the East Village.

The man Carolyn was living with was tall and thin, with dark eyes and straight black hair. His voice was tight, his manner condescending. There was something false about his bohemian air, and I didn't like him. I did like Carolyn. We spent most of the evening engrossed in getting to know each other. I learned that she had a love of lutes and literature, and discovered over the next few weeks that she was a shy romantic with a puritanical inner judge who stalked her like a demon. She gave me the impression of someone who had just stepped out of the eighteenth century into a 60s Greenwich Village street scene. She was slightly confused and constantly coping, doing her best to adapt and fit in with the crowd.

For a time, Carolyn was my best friend, and then I fell in love with her while trying to carry on a long-distance romance with Adin, a man I'd only known for thirty days. Common sense should have told me to let it go when he left for the West Coast, but I persisted in believing we were meant to be together. It may have been because he looked like Adonis, or because the hours we spent naked together had been filled with pleasure. Perhaps I was clinging to the notion that loving women was a transitory state on my way to the wedding my mother had always wanted for me. Whatever the reason, or maybe for all those reasons, I ended up following Adin to California. I called to let him know I was on my way and he said he would meet me at the airport. I waited there for what seemed an eternity, until he finally showed up. He was drugged out, drained, haggard. And already involved with another woman. End of fantasy.

Not long after I closed that disastrous chapter in my life, Carolyn left the man she'd been with for three years and came to San Francisco. I picked her up at the airport and she stayed with me. We knew where it was headed; we had tentatively discussed our feelings for each other one twilight evening in New York. At the time, we were both trying to make other relationships work, so we simply held hands and held on to our friendship. Now everything had changed, except that we were still attracted to one another. I made love to her and after that, everything became hopelessly complex.

We lived together for a year and a half. In the sweet abandon of youth and new love, we pooled our money and resources and made our way to Big Sur. We rented a modest cabin that was only available during the off-season, September through May. The cabin was sheltered by redwoods, situated on a gentle slope above the Big Sur River. It was two rooms and a bathroom, sufficient to meet our needs. In the kitchen, we cooked, ate, and visited with friends when they came by. A big room with windows overlooking the river served as bedroom and study.

We were two writers who had committed our time to work. I was writing a play; Lauren was completing a children's book. Although we did work, I mainly remember our intense lovemaking and long talks, and arguments that locked us in verbal combat for hours on end. It was exhausting. There was an occasional brief respite when we were peaceful together, tiny islands in an ocean of emotional violence. But those islands were not enough to mend the relationship we shredded over the course of the winter.

We broke up by mutual agreement and found separate living arrangements once we were back in San Francisco. We became distant friends—a distance that grew because, for a long while, we seemed unable to understand or speak to each other on any terms.

It's now nearly four years since Carolyn and I broke up and we are, once again, friends. But of late, after spending time with her, I find that I'm sad and extremely tired. She indulges in nearly constant introspection, and her interior landscape is dominated by feelings of guilt, rejection and need. Her lighter moments are fleeting, like thin glimmers of blue in a clouded sky.

Once, in a moment of clarity, I heard Carolyn say, "I get off on not getting off." Statements like this renew my faith in her. I'm reminded of the person I was drawn to, the friend I loved. But I'm realizing that her observations about her own behavior, articulated with some humor, are also tidbits that keep me trapped in our odd dialogue. She has deduced that I'm more interested in health than neurosis, drawn to strength rather than weakness. And I've begun to understand that she has subtly, deftly, won me back into an ongoing drama—one in which I play the strong, clear woman to her weak, confused woman. In this drama, inevitably, I find I am either reassuring her or giving her advice. I've begun to recognize that our exchange is one in which she gets the attention and I get to be wise.

Carolyn often tells me that she wants a lover more than anything in the world. But invariably, her lovers are transitory; her affairs are intense and short-lived. It may be that she can't hold on to love because she doesn't allow herself to rest when she's in a relationship. She persists in measuring her partners, testing their ability to take her intensity, as if she had a constant need to know how the other person is responding to her.

When Carolyn states that she's a lesbian, she declares it with a fierceness I find embarrassing. The fact of being gay is still the scar on her fair ivory skin, the dent in the carefully crafted model of behavior that her parents instilled in her. But I don't know if accepting this aspect of herself is all there is to curing Carolyn of her neurosis. She seems addicted to pain, to a state of turmoil that is both internal and external. I don't understand it, and at times it infuriates me. But mainly, I am saddened that the beautiful and passionate woman I fell in love with in

New York is being submerged by a relentlessly unhappy personality.

From my vantage point on Telegraph Hill, with a wide vista from the Pacific Ocean to the Berkeley Hills across the bay, I look again at the trio of ripe persimmons so near to my touch, and the one high above them, all alone. Carolyn is like that tiny persimmon at the top of the tree, isolated, looking with longing at the ripe, warm gathering of others nearer the earth. She is the perfect potential of what it means to be a person, but she is stunted in her growth, and unfortunate in her location. I walk away from the persimmon tree, knowing that the one at the very top is too high to be picked. It will be fruit for the birds, or a shriveled offering to the approaching icy winter wind.

September 2010. Tuesday afternoon. I'm in my studio, leafing through journal pages and notes for this memoir in progress. While reading my description of Carolyn, I remember a sunny morning in the early '70s when she and I took a walk together in Sonoma. She had a brown-and-white mutt with her, part-bird dog, part-cocker spaniel. He trotted along beside us, content, his long ears flapping. At the time, Carolyn was newly involved and she was happy, full of plans for the future. She had moved in with a woman named Abigail, someone I knew through other friends. I respected Abigail, but had never been able to really connect with her.

Carolyn's dog stayed near us, sniffing at this and that, his short legs giving a slightly comical bearing to his gait. He made me think of the two wild kittens Carolyn had found under the redwoods in Big Sur. We took them in and they became a part of us, providing us with more loving stability than anything we could manage between us. Carolyn was good with animals. She spoke to them directly, simply, in a tone of voice that made her affection and love for them apparent. They weren't subjected to the intellectual jargon she was prone to use with most people. Instead, they remained connected to what was genuine and authentic in her—the person who had a loving heart and knew how to play, how to laugh.

By the time we spent that hour together in the sunlight, too much had changed since I had first known Carolyn and fallen in love with her. Her insecurity was like a dark wizard behind the curtain, causing her at times to grasp at those who loved her, at other times to attack them. The insecurity was both emotional and material. I wish now that I could have understood her better, been more tolerant of her circumstances. I wish I could have bridged the gap between the Carolyn I loved and the one steeped in anxiety and neurosis. But we can't undo the past, or change who we were at any given time. I have to accept that we were both young, both coping as best we could. Each of us was caught up in our own personal quest, attempting to comprehend the world and seeking our place in it.

The relationship with Abigail didn't last. Long after she and Carolyn had split up, I ran into Abigail and spent some time talking with her. Though she seemed different from me in so many ways, it turned out that Abigail and I shared similar feelings about life with Carolyn. We had both been wrung out and worn out by her insecurities.

Sometimes, pacing in my studio, I glimpse a poem Carolyn wrote for me when we lived together in Big Sur. I unearthed it in my last move, and took the time to place it on the wall across from my desk. In nine short lines that burn with love and clarity, the poem captures an essential throughline in my life. It has always made me feel *seen*.

As I think of Carolyn and this poem, I look out the window to a spread of jasmine, thick with deep green leaves. Along the branches, tiny white flowers are budding, defying the cool autumn wind and reminding me of spring. In spite of the wintry storms I lived through with Carolyn, I want to hold onto and remember the promise of her talent, her Nordic beauty, the April innocence in her voice when I first heard her sing.

> *Phoenix lady,*
> *I have seen you now*
> *a hundred times*
> *dust ashes from your wings*
> *(how fierce they burn,*
> *some of our dreams)*
> *turn*
> *and soar again,*
> *eyes fixed on the sun.*

ZEN MIND, ZEN MUSCLE

In 1965, I moved to Manhattan. There, as I had done most of my life, I kept a small stack of books by my bedside. I took every opportunity to curl up in a comfortable place and lose myself in one of them. I discovered James Baldwin and Henry Miller. I read J. R. R. Tolkien and Aldous Huxley. But mainly I kept company with plays, and with books about Zen Buddhism. Most of the books about Zen Buddhism were by Alan Watts.

I started reading Watts during my brief stay in Sausalito, a beautiful little city on the Marin side of the San Francisco Bay. Alan Watts used to come into the post office where I worked. It was the only civil service job I've ever had. It wasn't a bad gig; it paid a decent salary and it came with benefits, though I was then too young to appreciate them.

At the time, I was living with Madeline, a gifted comedienne with a great voice—she could really belt out a song. We had become involved during my final year of college, and I soon learned she was far more practical than I was; rather than continuing in the theatre, where money was sporadic, she concentrated on both of us finding and holding down jobs that could pay the rent.

We lived in a small, ordinary apartment in a nondescript building. It was situated on a side street at the edge of town. None of that mattered; we were still in Sausalito. The commute to my job took about five minutes, and I drove to work five days a week on Sausalito's main thoroughfare, a street called Bridgeway that runs along one of the most beautiful waterfronts on God's green earth. With all this at hand, one might think I would have lasted more than several months at the United States Postal Service. But a long-distance phone call changed the trajectory I was on and set me back on a path toward my true love—the theatre and performing arts in all its myriad forms.

The call was from friends who had moved to New York in 1963; they were writing an original revue and the wheels were in motion to have it produced. They wanted me to direct and they wanted Madeline in the cast. It was bound to be a hit—they were a talented duo and had already proved their mettle in San Francisco. At the end of summer 1965, Madeline and I headed for the bright lights, big city.

But before that happened, I was doing my best at the Sausalito Post Office, in what most people—including me—thought of as a real job. My first assignment was at the front counter, where I sold stamps and helped people with their various mailing needs, both domestic and international. I found it extremely stressful, since I never knew who I might have to wait on or what their mood might be on that particular day.

When I first waited on Alan Watts, I didn't know who he was. I'm not sure if I discovered his books on my own, or if I was led to them by a co-worker. What I noticed about Watts was that he spoke very little. He seemed off in another world, even though he was physically on *terra firma* with the rest of us. It wasn't until I moved to New York and turned on to grass and hashish that I realized he had probably been stoned.

It may have been drugs or the semblance of a meditative state, but whatever the reason for his aura of otherworldliness, Alan Watts—at least in his books—seemed to know about becoming enlightened, and I wanted in on the secret. No matter how much I read, I was never able to grasp what the *koans* were about, nor what Zen was about. It was a philosophy that fascinated me even as it continued to elude me.

After a year in New York, I traveled south to take a job as a theatre director in Fort Lee, Virginia. That lasted for about a year, and then I returned to New York. I began taking classes at an independent film school. My classes there covered the essentials, everything I needed to know in order to make my own—hopefully incredible—independent films. It was at this school that my photography teacher saved me from my ongoing and frustrating intellectual pursuit of Zen Buddhism. He was a tall, handsome black man with a compelling presence and an engaging sense of humor. One evening in class, we learned he was a student of Tai Chi, a Chinese discipline that neither I nor my classmates had ever heard of. When asked to explain Tai Chi, he indicated the rectangular table in front of him.

"What's the easiest way to move this table?" he asked. A couple of us offered suggestions. He listened, then stated, "The easiest way to move this table is to get somebody else to move it." We all looked at him, and he said, "That's Tai Chi."

It didn't explain Tai Chi to me, but still, it was a brilliant solution to the problem he had posed. I had a momentary feeling that I had heard a *koan* and actually understood it. I asked where he studied, and went to observe a class.

I found myself mesmerized by the slow-motion grace and fluidity of Tai Chi. I immediately signed up to take a class—this, I knew, was a discipline I had to learn.

I took to Tai Chi like an otter to water. I was in my element, and no longer had any need for the mental and philosophical mazes in Alan Watts' books on Zen. That centered state of being he wrote about, the quiet that had been my quest—I now felt I was experiencing it directly and physically—whenever I practiced Tai Chi. This was Zen in my muscles, Zen in the body and the body of Zen. I began a practice that has remained with me all these years. I will forever be grateful to the photography teacher who led me to Tai Chi.

NEW YORK, DIXIE, NEW YORK

Though I stopped reading Alan Watts when I discovered Tai Chi, three of the authors I continued to read—Carl Jung, Henry Miller, and J.R.R. Tolkien—all provided pathways to worlds that would remain important to me in the years to come. My time with Tolkien began with *The Hobbit,* closely followed by his *Lord of the Rings Trilogy.* Tolkien knew how to tell a great story, and his writing took me along on a wonderful adventure. I was so deep into Middle-Earth that when the hobbits came upon "oliphaunts," I thought to myself: Oh, that's what elephants used to be called. Then I laughed at the realization that—at least while reading him—Tolkien's world had become real to me; his fiction had become a historical account. The awareness lasted only for those few moments. I turned the page, and became willingly lost again in Middle-Earth.

If J. R. R. Tolkien fed my need for adventure, Henry Miller grounded me in the life of a writer. I discovered his *Tropic of Cancer* at about the same time I quit my day job as a secretary at NBC. It was a move that was partly inspired by reading Miller, but mainly, I left due to the utter boredom of my job and the one-down experience of working for a man who seemed to view me as a clerical non-entity. I decided it was time to wing it through the world any which way that was legal and didn't involve working in an office.

My path to NBC had been circuitous. During my first year in New York, I had a part-time job at an academic publishing house. My boss was a slender, soft-spoken man with dark brown hair. His name was Aldo, and I guessed his age to be somewhere between thirty and thirty-five. He was intelligent, kind, and seemed to love his work.

My hours at the publishing house were flexible, which allowed me the freedom to pursue a creative life. I auditioned to study acting with Uta Hagen at the HB Studio, and was accepted. She was a brilliant actress and an exceptional teacher; her lessons in technique and craft were invaluable. Apart from those lessons, I also marveled at her ability to critique the work each actor had done in their assigned scenes. Her critiques were never personal; it was always about the work.

The rest of my creative life was mainly given to directing two musical revues, both written by the talented trio of friends who had beckoned Madeline and me away from California. The revues had short, mildly successful runs, but neither of them led immediately to bigger and better things for any of us involved.

After that first foray into life in Manhattan and the New York theatre scene, I went south to Virginia to take a job as a theatre director for Special Services, the entertainment branch of the U.S. Army. Open to civilians, it was a position my parents had heard about and encouraged me to apply for; they then urged me to accept, once the position was offered. After all, wasn't theatre direction what I had been educated and trained for?

Once again, I found myself in a job with a decent salary and benefits. But this time, I was in a theatre instead of a post office, dealing with actors, technicians and stage hands instead of letters and packages. The people who turned up to audition or work backstage were mainly soldiers, the wives of soldiers, and the civilian personnel who worked on the base. A few of the soldiers had come from the theatre and intended to return to it when their stint in the Army was over.

My boss was a charming Italian, aptly named Rome. He was an accomplished pianist with wavy black hair and a broad smile. Like me, he was a civilian. His suits were well-cut and his ties carefully chosen; his nails were manicured and his black leather shoes always had a hard shine. He was all about looking good and putting on a good show. My job was to direct the plays he chose and to help him with the entertainment events he created. Rome's showmanship and the few friends I made among the actors and backstage people made it possible, for a while, to survive in a small Southern town where there was nothing to see and nowhere to go. I went to work each day in a theatre that was part of a military base, where the predominant color scheme was brown, beige, and olive drab. After the beat and throb and excitement of New York, I felt as if I was in No Man's Land.

Madeline was still living in New York. Our friendship had held fast, but we were no longer a couple—Madeline loved me, but her nature was to be with men, just as mine is to be with women. She took the bus to visit me just once while I was in Virginia, and she talked me into driving her back to Manhattan for a brief hit of Christmas in the Big Apple. I ended up with only a few hours in the city, and I have a vivid memory of walking into a trendy, upscale store on Fifth Avenue and standing in the entryway, transfixed. It was the first time I had seen those tiny white lights we now see everywhere at Christmastime. The entire store was strung with thousands of lights, and there was stereophonic sound playing up-tempo music that made me want to dance. The lights had been preset to flash to the beat of the music. It was all so elegant, so grand, so *turned on*, that I wept.

I think it was the only time I let myself feel how much I missed New York. Though I didn't articulate it, that experience made me realize I wasn't going to last in my financially comfortable exile. I didn't let myself think about it or try to make any decisions. It turned out I didn't have to. Soon into the new year, Rome left for another position in Chicago. When his replacement arrived, I knew the end was in sight. My new boss was a trim, middle-aged woman with hennaed red hair. She did everything by the book, including wearing the blue-gray Special Services uniform. She let it be known that I would also be required to wear the uniform. Every day. That was a bridge too far. I quit.

I returned to New York and got a job as a secretary for the unit production managers overseeing *The Tonight Show*. I had been encouraged to seek work in television by a friend in Virginia, an ambitious young man who had worked in radio and fully intended to make a career as a broadcaster. He had made a convincing case for the small screen, and he was certainly right about jobs being available. I showed up to work each day at what is now known as Rock Center. I was a secretary for a unit production manager—one of several secretaries for several unit production managers. The secretaries were all women, the managers were all men.

Though it wasn't the theatre—my first love—I held on to the possibility that a modest beginning in television would eventually lead to a position that placed me in the company of writers and directors, and a chance to work with people I admired and hoped to know. I was only in the general vicinity of those people when I took advantage of the major benefit of my job—every afternoon I was able to watch the "talent" rehearse for the Tonight Show scheduled for that evening. I was lucky enough to see some incredible musicians and singers, but that was as close as I got to the show business aspect of my time at NBC. My job was dull. I was typing, filing, and answering phones for a group of men who seemed to view the women in the office as useful décor. I may have been changing my outfit every day, but I was still wearing a uniform.

At about the time that I had this realization, I was also reading Henry Miller. Maybe it was just what I wanted to hear, but Miller seemed to be telling me to stand up and step out of the safe boat I was riding in; he was exhorting me to plunge into the great buoyant ocean of creative endeavor, whatever that endeavor might be. NBC was the boat, and the endeavor I wanted to undertake was a play about racism. The civil rights movement, coupled with my own experiences in the South, was causing this issue to occupy a central place in my thoughts.

While wondering if I could or should leave a job I hated, my friend Gary made me an offer. He had been getting nowhere writing serious plays, and he told me he had finally gotten somewhere by writing a soft-porn screenplay. He had secured the money to produce his script, which meant there was enough money to pay everyone involved, actors and crew. He was directing, and he asked if I wanted to be his assistant during the filming. It was only a few weeks of work, but it still looked like my meal ticket out of NBC, and I took it.

I met some good people and enjoyed myself working on Gary's film. For one thing, I quickly remembered that I was more than a competent typist. I knew how to work with actors, and I could improvise and come up with solutions for the odd problems and varied situations that came up during production. Not long after we completed filming, Gary told me he had seen the future and this was it: there was money to be made in soft-porn films. He had decided to form a company, and he wanted me to be part of it. He told me it could eventually lead to directing, if that's what I wanted, and he assured me that accepting his offer didn't preclude working on my play or other serious writing—it just meant I could pursue that work and have enough money to eat regularly and pay the rent.

I thanked him, and declined. It may have been Gary's future, but I didn't want it to be mine. Though it was unlike anything I had ever done before, it seemed to me that dealing with soft-porn material on a daily basis would ultimately be as limiting as the family-friendly plays I had directed for Special Services in Virginia.

I lived on the little I had managed to save, and kept on reading Henry Miller. I was caught up in his enormous appetite for life—food, women, Paris, language, friendship—he consumed it all, ever-hungry for more. I shared his passion, the beat of his writer's heart. All during my last year in New York, I was writing my life in New York. No matter what my experience on any given day, I got it on paper at night, settling in with my portable Hermes typewriter around midnight and pounding out the pages before going to sleep in the pre-dawn hours.

THE ROAD TO CARL JUNG COUNTRY

While Henry Miller connected me to earth and earthly appetites, Carl Jung quenched my soul-thirst. He spoke to the place in me that was in love with the mysterious and mystical realm of the psyche. While reading Jung's *Memories, Dreams, Reflections,* I became absorbed in the inner-other world of dreams and mythology, and I was introduced to a whole new vocabulary: alchemy, individuation, transfiguration, synchronicity. This was a rich, multidimensional universe.

When I think of Jung's life story, the image that comes to mind is of a lake discovered while walking in the forest, a lake much like the one he describes in the opening pages of his book: "The lake stretched away and away into the distance. This expanse of water was an inconceivable pleasure to me, an incomparable splendor." Carl Jung's reflections revealed a shimmering body of water that called to me, inviting me to explore new and intriguing concepts. I waded in and kept going, kept swimming, until I had reached the far shore. And even at that far shore, having turned the last page, I had not reached the end. Though I didn't know it at the time, my journey with Jung would continue long after I left New York.

It was while I was reading Jung that I met and became friends with an astrologer, Rod Chase. Rod introduced me to the signs and symbols of the zodiac, their relationships and meaning, and he told me about my own sign and the significance of Scorpio, a sign identified with death, sex, and regeneration. In my chart he saw an aspect of me that I had never considered: the archetype of the Healer.

"You are a healer," he said. "You have healing power."

I didn't know what to do with that. I simply put it at the back of my mind and left it there to brew, to see what would become of it, if anything. At about this same time, I discovered Arthur Ford's book, *Nothing So Strange*. I began experimenting with the notion of having psychic abilities. I took careful notes, tried some of the exercises that Ford proposed, and on occasion had some startling experiences. Like Carl Jung's world of the psyche, this was both new and vaguely familiar—my grandmother Romana could read the cards and tell your fortune (she used an ordinary playing deck, no Tarot for her)—and my mother often had precognitive dreams.

During this time, I was living with Madeline again, in a relationship that had been redefined: we were ex-lovers who had remained friends. She had started seeing a clean-cut young man who—in look, style and interests—seemed the direct opposite of our on-the-fringe theatre crowd. He may have been Madeline's way of gaining distance from the ultra-closeted world she and I had been living in, her attempt to "normalize" her life by being part of a male-female couple who looked more like the '50s than our own raucous decade, the freewheeling '60s.

Not to be left home alone, I got briefly involved with a painter named Brant. We met one evening at an outdoor rock concert in Tompkins Square Park. He had brought a bottle of wine and we began sharing it and talking. He was brawny and voluble, a bull of a man with wild, curly hair and a deep voice. I liked his vivid stories; one of them was about the way he had busted loose from his staid Midwestern life to come to New York and stake everything on his art.

The affair with Brant lasted little more than a month. During that time, he introduced me to some of his favorite places in the East Village. One of these, the Odessa Café, served a hearty bowl of borscht for a quarter, every day of the week. Whenever money was tight, which was often, that soup helped me stay alive. Brant also taught me how to roll a joint, or a cigarette, if one were inclined toward tobacco. He was serious about my lesson; he made me practice until I got it just right.

Though he claimed to be all about freedom, Brant became possessive fairly quickly, and I felt less and less free with him. The volatility that at first had made it exciting to be with him soon began to feel like living on the edge of a cliff: precarious. I heard warning bells telling me to get clear of him before some lethal mix of drugs, alcohol and temper made him push me off that cliff. When I broke up with him, he was at first sarcastic, then mean. I walked away when he started hurling insults, and I went back to the small West Village apartment I shared with Madeline.

Madeline was at home, and I told her what had happened with Brant. I was hoping his verbal abuse marked an end to the affair, but about an hour later, someone was knocking at the door. I indicated to Madeline that we should stay quiet and not answer. The knocking turned into a loud banging, and then we heard Brant, insisting that I was there, demanding to be let in. When we didn't respond, he let all his craziness explode. Madeline and I stayed absolutely silent while he banged and bellowed at the door. It went on for a long time, but he finally gave up. When we found the courage to open the door, we saw a sheaf of peacock feathers that he had left behind. Madeline told me they were meant to bring bad luck. I shuddered at the sight of them, grateful that the door had held.

There was no repeat performance. It was a strange interlude, one I didn't try to analyze. Looking back, I remember the pain I felt whenever Madeline went off to spend her nights with her well-tailored young man, pain I tried to minimize. Brant was lusty and loud; he had given me a way to divert the tide of sadness that threatened to swamp me. I may have needed a raft to cling to, but in Brant, I had chosen badly.

About fifteen years later, I encountered him again. I was with friends in North Beach; we were on our way to City Lights bookstore. There on the street, walking toward us, was Brant. He saw me and broke into a familiar grin, revealing rotting teeth. He wore dusty old jeans and a frayed shirt. There were beads around his neck and a wide bracelet on his wrist. He had been ravaged by drugs, but he still swaggered. He said I probably wouldn't want to have anything to do with him now, then spoke proudly of stealing sacred objects from Native American burial grounds. I didn't know if it was true or if he just wanted to shock me. I hoped he was lying but suspected he wasn't. I wished him well and walked on.

Madeline had been saving money for a long while so she could travel, and in the fall of 1967, she left for Europe. I was on my own, deconstructing and reconstructing my life. America seemed to be doing the same. I was, at times, a cool observer of the changes I saw going on all around me. At other times, I was a passionate participant in those changes. I was filled with misery about the war in Vietnam. I joined anti-war protests and marches; I attended a draft card-burning in Central Park where Joan Baez sang and spoke to the crowd. These events did little to alleviate my sense of feeling powerless. The war went on.

It was after Madeline left for Europe that I met Carolyn, and then Adin. Adin and I became lovers. The time with him was sweet, but he was uncertain about making a life on the East Coast, and he went back to California. With only letters to connect us, my misgivings about him began to surface. Still, I held on to the memory of our romance.

In the spring of '68, while walking along a street in the Village, I looked up at the trees beginning to blur into green. I had a sudden longing to immerse myself in green—I wanted meadows and hills and grassy valleys, forest groves and wooded glens. I felt weary of cement and the harshness of my life in the city. I was tired of my long-distance relationship with Adin; I wanted to be with him. I wanted California.

Though the relationship with Adin didn't work out, following him to California eventually led me to the road I was meant to be on, the one that took me to Carl Jung country: Sonoma County. That road opened up to me after Carolyn and I decided to leave each other and Big Sur. We returned to San Francisco and each of us embarked on separate lives.

I was still winging my way with odd and sundry jobs, and for a while I was a sidewalk artist-vendor, selling my rice-paper paintings on a pleasant street that edged Aquatic Park in the Marina District of the city. The block where I set up my wares was across from the Buena Vista Café, famous for its Irish coffee. One sunlit day when I was hawking—in my own quiet way—my multicolored creations, I saw a woman I knew from my Drama Department days at San Francisco State. Ellyn was walking toward me, smiling, arms outstretched to embrace me. It had been at least five years since we had last seen each other. We were both theatre people and easily renewed a friendship that had not quite developed when we went in different directions after college.

Ellyn had beautiful eyes and long, light-brown hair. She was slender, confident, and moved with ease in a world she believed to be in transition to the new Age of Aquarius. What attracted me most to Ellyn was her dazzling intellect—the tumble and flow of ideas that were her daily fare, and her constant search for ways to translate new concepts into the ritual of theatre. She also seemed fluent in a language I recognized from reading Jung—she talked often about dreams, myth, and exploring creativity through archetypes and the shadow self, the *animus* and *anima*.

We were soon lovers, spending time together at every opportunity that the miles between us would allow—she was on the faculty at Sonoma State and lived near the campus, an hour or more from where I was living in San Francisco. I was enthralled with her, and she with me; it was not long after we became involved that she asked me to come live with her. I packed up my few belongings and moved to Santa Rosa.

Not long after I moved in, a few of Ellyn's friends came by the house—one of them was a woman named Dru. At that first meeting, and the few times when I saw her again, I found that Dru seemed to treat me with a certain subtle hostility. I never thought to ask Ellyn about it, perhaps because I was uncertain if the "vibe" coming from Dru was real or imaginary. It was from someone who had known both Ellyn and Dru for a long time that I learned the truth: Dru had been ousted from Ellyn's house in order to make room for me. I knew then that the undercurrent of hostility I was feeling was real.

After about a year, there was another undercurrent in the household—one I didn't understand and couldn't articulate. Long before I knew that there was a term for it, I had a sense of being discounted. I was too naive to realize Ellyn's interest had cooled and I stayed on, trying to make the relationship work. I didn't comprehend the slights and verbal digs coming my way, and I endured some real emotional misery before finally coming to grips with the deep unhappiness I was experiencing.

The relationship ended a year and some months later, and I came out of it with my self-confidence deeply shaken. I took on the difficult task of trying to mend my broken heart and restore my ego. Fortunately, I was in the right place to remake and recreate myself; Sonoma County was at the center of the New Age movement and, at Sonoma State, one could delve deeply into a study of the self.

The Psychology Department at the college had an impressive faculty, and I would soon be part of the master's program there. But I began my foray into academia at the Humanistic Psychology Institute, which was situated on the Sonoma State campus. I felt at home with the people there, and comfortable with the subjects we discussed, the books we were reading, and the ideas we were exploring. It was there that I met Ann, who would encourage me to pursue a graduate degree. What lay beyond the far shore of that lake I had discovered while reading Carl Jung was here in Sonoma, a place where I could study the science of the soul. Here it was possible to forge meaning and a larger narrative from one's personal story.

TAI CHI AND TRANSITION

I had been practicing Tai Chi for several years by the time I moved to Sonoma. I had also studied with two teachers, Tam Gibbs in New York and Joseph Lee at the Chinese Community Center in San Francisco. Joseph Lee is the man whom I will forever consider my true teacher. Watching him demonstrate the Tai Chi forms in class was like looking into pure, crystal-clear water. The fluidity, grace, and simplicity of his motions embodied, for me, the essence of Tai Chi.

A few friends who had watched me do Tai Chi were drawn to it and began asking me to teach them. There seemed to be no one else in the vicinity who knew Tai Chi; I was it. I began teaching a few people and, gradually, my classes became larger and more numerous. I held classes in scattered locations around the county, traveling in my old VW bug. With some breaks in between to write a book, teach theatre, direct, and work with a couple of "right livelihood" organizations, I went on to teach Tai Chi for a dozen years, with classes in Sonoma

County and the San Francisco Bay Area and, later on, in Los Angeles.

Teaching Tai Chi was a joy. Becoming a teacher also caused me reflect on the learning process. I took note especially of people who were self-conscious. Their self-consciousness made them tense, the opposite of the relaxed state that characterizes the forms and motions of Tai Chi. I sought ways to make my students feel safe, and experimented with methods of making the learning process easier. I wanted to communicate clearly, and to impart Tai Chi not only as a physical discipline, but as a way of being. Looking back, it might have been Watts-like of me to think in those terms, but it was the tenor of the times, and it was also the truth. The origins of Tai Chi are rooted in Taoism; Tai Chi is a physical expression of Taoist principles. I had understood instinctively from the first that Tai Chi was more than a beautiful way to move.

Along with my love of Tai Chi, my interest in metaphysics and psychic abilities had continued unabated ever since reading Arthur Ford. The summer before I began the graduate program at Sonoma State, I spotted a book called *Psychic Discoveries Behind the Iron Curtain*. It was fascinating; it triggered in me a number of ideas about learning, healing, and consciousness.

One of my classes was at Sonoma State Hospital, a psychiatric facility where I taught Tai Chi to members of the staff. The experience there caused me to think about the physical space that served as a residence for the mentally ill. It seemed barren, a place that deadened the spirit and dulled the mind. It was hard to imagine anyone getting well in such a cold and unimaginative environment.

My trips to the hospital may have been why I was particularly interested in a section of *Psychic Discoveries* that dealt with the effects of various non-rectangular spaces. It was my introduction to the idea that certain geometric structures might help people become more centered and aware: physical space could have a healthful effect. I began to consider all the elements that could help or hinder healing, and realized I had found my master's thesis.

Without seeking it, I had also found my identity as healer. I had never wanted to be a doctor, never wanted to be a therapist, but I cared about people who were ill, and I was forming ideas about certain factors that might ease suffering and aid healing. If I had anything to contribute to the field I was studying, anything to contribute to the healing arts, it was this: medicine is not only in pills or fluids; therapy is not only in the verbal exchange between patient and therapist. Every element in one's environment can be intentionally designed or used to aid the mysterious process of healing.

In our twenty-first century, people are familiar with Feng Shui, the power of place, and the concept of "healing design." But in the early '70s, when I wrote the manuscript that would become *The Healing Environment*, I had ventured into unchartered territory. Perhaps my healing power lay in my ability to create a map for others.

I had continued to read Henry Miller since living in New York and—during this period of exploring the concept of place and healing—I would learn about and eventually meet Anais Nin, a writer who had been an important part of Miller's life. At the end of my relationship with Ellyn, I had not only moved out of her house, I had also distanced myself from people close to her. I made a new circle of friends. One of them was Geri, a wonderfully spirited and intelligent woman who was an early advocate for the art and writing of women in general, and of certain women in particular. Geri introduced me to the work of Anais Nin. I began reading her diaries, and found in her writing an elegant mind and a richly detailed chronicle of her life in another era.

At about the time that I completed reworking my thesis into a book-length manuscript, Anais Nin was invited to speak at Sonoma State. I was there at the talk she gave, one of many in the large audience who admired her. Geri had been instrumental in arranging and coordinating this visit, and she knew I shared her enthusiasm for Ms. Nin's work, so I was one of the fortunate few who had the opportunity to spend an evening with her at Geri's home.

Anais Nin was still beautiful, though frail. She was battling cancer, and had been subject to the debilitating effects of radiation. I spoke with her about my belief in the therapeutic effects of place and told her about my manuscript. She was intrigued, and interested in reading it. I sent the manuscript to her, and still have the letter she wrote to me after reading it. An excerpt from her letter appears on the back cover of the book: "*The Healing Environment*...touches one humanly and clarifies truths which would be less effective told in an abstract way as ideas. I love it and I believe every word… You arouse many speculations, reveries, and the desire to act…"

Anais Nin died in 1977, a year after the book was published.

The years in Sonoma marked a major transition in my life. One essential element in that transition was that this Northern California region was profoundly welcoming: I found a whole community of people there who met me on my own terms, without judgment. It was my first experience of living in a place where it was okay to be gay. Before moving to Sonoma, I had been in the closet. Outside of a select group of friends, I had kept my personal life hidden. But now I was with people who viewed sexuality and its varied expressions as simply another aspect of the human experience. Buoyed by the aura—and actuality—of acceptance, I found the courage to come out to my mother.

I was living with Stephanie, out in the countryside, in one-half of a duplex in Sebastopol. Stephanie was away until dinner-time and my mother, who lived in Oakland, had come to visit. We were talking, sitting together in a narrow living room with windows that looked out over a rural road. I'm not sure anymore what the preamble was or what prompted me, that particular afternoon, to tell my mother that Stephanie and I weren't roommates—I loved her, and she loved me.

There was a moment of silence while my mother took in what I had just told her, a moment when she began adjusting to this new understanding of my life with Stephanie. Then she said, "You make your bed, and you lie in it."

Just that, nothing more. I think she was sad for me, because she realized it was not an easy path I had taken. She knew that most of the world would be against me, that many people would consider me odd, or sick, or sinful. It was, I believe, her awareness of the difficulties I faced as a gay woman that made her sad. But I was still her daughter, and she didn't treat me any differently than she had before I made my declaration. She never judged me, never asked me to make a different choice, never stopped loving me.

I didn't think about it at the time, but it was probably then, on that cloud-gray afternoon, that she gave up on the one thing she had been hoping for since I had rounded the curve from girlhood into womanhood—my wedding.

HEADLINE

IT'S OFFICIAL: GAYS ARE SANE. That was the headline. There it was at last, in December 1973. The American Psychiatric Association had ruled that homosexuality is not a sickness.

I came out to my friend Patience, twenty years my senior, while discussing the Gays Are Sane headline. I still remember her response to my disclosure, her visible discomfort. We were sitting together in the spacious living room of her hillside home, a view of the San Francisco Bay below us. She was drinking a gin and tonic, her evening cocktail. I watched her fingers tap the tall glass. She was silent for a moment, struggling with her emotions. "I can't help it," she admitted. "My background ... has always made me think of it as a distortion."

A distortion. Long before Patience used that word to describe her view of homosexuality, it had been imprinted in me by the Catholic Church. As I was entering adulthood, struggling between what was expected of me and what I wanted, it was the Church's condemnation that I feared. It was the Catholic Church that had me crippled in the grip of its sainted embrace.

I felt that grip as an embrace because I had spent my childhood constantly moving, constantly adapting. I was an Army brat, and life was a series of new schools and new friends, new houses in new cities. There was little I could count on to remain fixed for any length of time. Being Catholic was part of my stability. It was my religious ground. When I first began to recognize that I was drawn to women, I felt that ground break, split, and then open like a chasm beneath me.

In college, I had a friend named Peter who longed to dance. In the world of theatre, he found that his talent was welcome. His feelings for other men were accepted. But in the world where he had grown up, those feelings were neither discussed nor tolerated. In spite of that intolerance, Peter still yearned to remain in the familiar shelter that had been his in childhood, a place where he had the blessing of his parents, his family, his church. To obtain that blessing, he gave up on being a dancer. He married and moved away from his friends. When the marriage and his other sacrifices did nothing to diminish his attraction to men, he bit down even harder on the bone that Christianity offered and subjected himself to aversion therapy. After I heard about it, I wept.

I had directed Peter in a play, and had often found myself stunned by his presence on stage. There was something true in the way he moved, a fluidity that had both grace and power. I marveled at the quality and depth he brought to a role. He was unique, gifted. When

I thought of him in aversion therapy, I imagined Peter forcing himself to endure sickening sensations, being made to associate those sensations with images that had once brought him pleasure. To what end, other than to twist his beauty and talent into self-loathing?

Aversion therapy in all its forms was a concerted and cruel campaign to make straight what tended to curve, to close what was meant to be open. It was this puritanical dictum that created the real distortion: men and women trying to break their bodies into shapes that fit the prescribed norm, trying to bend their feelings into a semblance of emotions that were acceptable to a narrow and grievously intolerant society.

I was lucky. I followed my heart. As the massive tree that was the Catholic Church crumbled and fell away, I clung to a branch. That branch was my faith, my own vision and understanding of God. The branch turned out to be an impenetrable oak that was rooted deep inside me.

Though it took nearly a decade, I came to terms with my sexuality before the APA declared me normal. I knew who I was and I had accepted the fact that I was part of a sexual minority. But in December 1973, I became an official card-carrying member of the sane majority. Two years before the APA made its ruling, I was living with Ellyn, in her house up in the hills of Santa Rosa. It was on a rural road that wound down to the campus of Sonoma State. I had just begun the preliminary courses that would later lead to my graduate work there. I remember a cold, gray afternoon when I set my books aside and decided to tackle the blackberry bushes that had grown rampant at the side of the house. They were taking over, covering everything in a snarl of thick, thorny vines.

March 1971. Tuesday afternoon. The blackberries at the creek side of the house are greedy for all the water, all the light, all the land. I hack, and cut, and the blackberry branches fall. As I clear each successive area, the earth exhales. Her breath is like mint, sweet, and good. All the forgotten little plants, suffocating for so long beneath the weight of the blackberries, seem to be saying thank you, thank you. Thank you for the light. Thank you for the air.

I rest from my labors and remember myself as a girl. I think that I must have been like this fragrant garden before the thorny vines engulfed it—beautiful, playful, stretching toward the sky, filled with energy and in love with life. I didn't know what sin was. The Church had to describe sin and teach me what it meant. And her sons and daughters, the priests and the nuns, took up their charge and carried it out with a vengeance. Sister Dominic, her tall, bony frame full of strength and furious intelligence, all wrapped up in God, pounding history into our heads. "Wake up!" she would yell. "Wake up!" Slapping her ruler hard against the desk—thunder and lightning in the guise of a Sister of Charity.

Wake up! This is the world, child. This is the way it is. The nuns and the priests told me what sin was and defined it in detail. They told me which were the minor sins and which were the major sins. *Mea culpa, mea culpa, mea culpa.* The thorny vines multiplied, grew thick and strong in the sweet, wild garden, twisting together into a dense network of distorted thoughts. As the months and years went by, the thorns of guilt grew sharper, cut deeper. Centuries of patriarchy. Huge tomes written by men. And I was supposed to carry that weight for a lifetime.

I hack at the thorny vines and watch them fall, and I rejoice with the earth and the plants released to the air, to the light.

AWAKENING

It was summer, 1962. I was in Mexico, traveling with a young man who had always wanted to see this country. Tall and lanky, with a trim, blond beard and a deep voice, Reid was a philosophy student and a photographer, and my first lover.

We had been on the road, headed uphill, for several hours, and by late afternoon we were in the mountains north of Mexico City. The stifling heat was now far below us. Near sunset, we stopped at a modest inn. As I stepped out of the car, I felt a gentle breeze that was cool, fresh. If I lived in this country, I thought, it would be in these mountains.

The inn was simple and clean. The man who owned it spoke English, as did his wife, though she was not nearly as fluent. They led us to a terrace that looked out over an incredible vista. While his wife brought us food and drink, our host sat with us and spoke of the lore of these mountains. Filled with a sense of his own importance, he told us about his family and this inn that had been built by his grandfather. He addressed himself mainly to Reid, demanding all his attention. I sat in silence, watching his wife serve us with a graciousness that was inherent, natural. I thanked her, and noted that her husband ignored her.

How, I wondered, could he be so dismissive of this beautiful woman? She was slender and graceful, with dark brown eyes and a wonderful smile. I looked at her thick, black hair, the lustrous waves that fell around her face and shoulders, a few strands lifted now and then by the breeze. How was it possible that her husband could take her for granted, and relegate her to the background? There was nothing in his manner to indicate affection or appreciation. It was as if he had ceased to notice her.

As she walked away from the table, I sensed that she had not yet grown accustomed to being ignored. Something in the way she carried herself showed me that she still remembered who she was, still remembered being courted and adored. Was that sense of herself being erased in the day-to-day company of an egotistical husband? Would she soon forget that she was beautiful, desirable?

I felt a wave of emotion wash over me, so strong that it eclipsed everything around me. The voices of the two men faded, and the mountain view, the twilight sky—all of it disappeared. I saw only this woman on the terrace, and I wanted to hold her, make love to her, and tell her in a thousand ways how lovely she was.

It was the first time I had ever thought of making love to a woman. And in that moment, it was more than a thought. The sensation was physical, visceral, sublime. My heart was full and my arms ached. With every fiber of my being, I wanted to love this woman who was, in that instant, every woman. I wanted to soothe every slight, heal every hurt she had experienced. I wanted to give her all the tenderness one human being can give to another.

The moment passed. Politeness intervened, and I was drawn back to the discussion at the table, back to reality. But in those few seconds I recognized in myself a capacity to love that was all-encompassing. And that understanding had been awakened by a woman.

WHERE IT BEGAN

Late November, 1974. Inexplicably sad this morning. Bright sunlight and blue winter sky above San Francisco, but my mood is tear-filled. I drive up to Buena Vista Park, back to the neighborhood where I lived for a while in my student days. I walk to the two-story house where I had my first solitary dwelling, a place that I rented for twenty-five dollars a month. That sum bought me a big room that was bedroom, living room and study all in one, and a tiny kitchen with a window that looked out over the rooftops. Out in the hallway, there was a bathroom with a shower that I shared with the studio apartment next door. Perhaps best of all, I had a small balcony to call my own, where I would sometimes sit at twilight and play my guitar.

I love this quiet, clean street with its fine old houses, flowering gardens, and graceful trees. I stand out on the sidewalk and look up at the house that I once called home. In my mind, I step through the big balcony window, open to the room filled with so many memories.

In that room I lost my virginity to a gentle young man who studied philosophy, played classical guitar, and took fine black-and-white photographs of people and places he loved. There I wrote a play that was produced and toured for a season throughout the Bay Area, bringing me some income to fund my student life. I wrote it sitting at a desk that was a solid piece of plywood resting on two old filing cabinets. The filing cabinets and the plywood had been provided by my half-brother Bill. Nine years my senior, Bill had grown up in a separate household. It was only as a young adult that I began to know him, and to enjoy his inventiveness and generous spirit. I spent long hours at the desk he had fashioned for me, chewing on pencils, smoking an occasional cigarette, sipping scotch from a small glass tumbler.

In that room I studied, and slept, and wondered on the future. I made hot buttered rum for my friends at Christmastime, and wrapped small presents for them in a bonanza of multi-colored tissue paper. And while I lived in this good place, I made love with a woman for the first time.

Aurelia was a friend and a fellow drama student. Both of us were talented and in love with the theatre; we shared a world of similar ideals and aspirations. When I recognized that our bond of friendship was tinged with desire, I was brave enough to confess my feelings for her.

Her response to my confession was both yes–and–no. She told me that she loved me, and sometimes she let me hold her. But she kept reiterating that she needed a man in her life. Then, while I was away on winter break, she left a note for me, and exquisite gifts. She wrote that she had thought about it for a long time, struggled and cried over what I was asking of her. At the end of it all, she was left only with the fact of her love for me. The essence of her note was consent, consent to let me love her and make love to her.

Her gifts moved me. Her invitation thrilled me. Still, I waited. Making love to a woman was new to me. But what I felt for her was clear; in my imagination I had traveled this territory before.

It was during that waiting period that the imagined territory became *terra firma*. She came to see me one evening and helped me with the small tasks my neighbors down the hall had asked of me while they were away on a trip. We watered their plants, then stayed to enjoy the comfortably furnished space. The amenities included a television, something neither of us could afford to own. As we sat close together on the ample sofa in front of the small screen, I knew it was time—time to stop listening to her say I-love-you-but-I-have-to-have-a-man. Some kind of demon-angel overtook me and I seduced her. In the heat and tumult of our passion and pleasure, she called my name, and our nights of frustrated wrestling were over.

BETWEEN THE JEWELS

I haven't told you about the pomegranate. Mainly because I've been dwelling on persimmons, with their pure orange hue and sweet, soft taste of pleasure. The pomegranate is another story. It has a hard, leathery skin that encases a treasure of deep red jewels, a cosmos of beauty. But the pulp between the jewels is bitter.

Autumn 1974. In my Gladys Street apartment in San Francisco, the day begins in jeweled crimson sweetness, with Stephanie pulling me close. Stephanie, who won me with good coffee and makes no promises, envelops me in her warmth and makes love to me. When I rise from the bed, I feel soft, whole. Everything in me bends toward her. Then, as we cook breakfast together, she tells me that she wants to spend the night away and asks if that's all right. She isn't asking for permission. She's asking only how I feel about her decision to spend the evening with someone else, a woman named Nora.

What I feel is that I have been opened only to receive a body blow that sends a stabbing pain through every part of me. I want to fold and fall to my knees, to lie crumpled on the floor until the misery that has taken hold loosens its grip. Instead, I remain upright, but I cannot hold back the tears. I cry and confess that I'm hurt. I spill my fears. Stephanie listens. She says, very gently, that Nora is expecting her this evening. And perhaps it will be just that—an evening away. I remind myself that I need to accept that it may be more. The freedom to be with other people is what we've agreed to, the reason we're living apart.

When the door has closed and Stephanie is gone, the bitter pulp of the pomegranate is an endlessly long day that I spend alone, quiet, moving slowly, like an animal tending her wounds. The bitterness is Stephanie's call near midnight, saying that she wants to stay where she is tonight, with Nora. This is hard, I tell her. I feel my heart breaking and I fight for control. Yes, I tell her. Yes. Stay with Nora. We say good night. I sit there and listen to the silence, then realize it is not silence. The radio is on and Bob Dylan is singing, "... *where are you tonight, sweet Marie?*"

It is the pomegranate that ages us, the hard reality of the crimson skin that wears us down. It is the acrid taste of the inner pulp between the sweet, clustered berries that makes me feel like an old woman as I write. And I know, when I look in the mirror, I will be shocked to see the deep lines carved into my face, the gray hair crowding the dark field of my youth.

SARA

Winter 1974. Sunday morning. I look out at a cold December sun lighting a yellow rose. I'm nostalgic, lonely. In love. I am in love with Stephanie, and with Sara. The avocado leaves are silhouetted against the last whispers of fog, and Paul Horn is in ecstasy, riding the music of his flute into endless sky. Sara stayed the night with me. This morning I woke up in her arms. She wrapped herself around me, gathered me in.

She has gone and I'm alone in Ernesto's home, on a quiet street in Petaluma. I've settled here temporarily, rent-free, in a many-windowed room at the back of the house. I have work and research to do at the college for the next few weeks. Ernesto's generosity means I don't have to spend endless hours on the freeway, driving back and forth between the college and my place in San Francisco. I love this room that is mine for a short while. There's a view of trees and a ramshackle shack at the end of a gravel drive, bordered by shrubbery and our neighbors' fence. At a slight distance, I can see their small Victorian house.

I have decided to undo the chaos Ernesto has left everywhere in the house. I spoke with him about it, and he's given me free rein to sort and clean to my heart's content. I am determined to rearrange the scatter of objects and books and paper into a semblance of order. Ernesto—dear curly-haired man who is so incredibly impractical and wonderful. Always wine in the house. Perhaps no food, but always wine. It's all right. I bring in the food.

Last night I became aware of Sara across the room, watching me. I was looking at the avocado plant by the window, deeply absorbed in the color of the leaves, the graceful pattern of shadow and light on the broad-leaf shape.

"What is it?" she asked. "What's going on?"

How to explain? Often now, this feeling comes over me. Suddenly, my perception clears and I see the essence and soul of objects. The shrubs along the fence, the avocado, the wood frame of the window. These everyday things, so beautiful. I feel on the edge of infinity, merging into a timeless state of joy. Ecstasy. Exaltation. Longing. These are the feelings that well up and wash over me as I move through my ordinary, extraordinary world. I contemplate the weave and pattern of the carpet on the floor beside my bed. I walk through the house and look at the plants, the perfect lamps, the arc of the windows at the front of the house, the glint of reflected light on the river in the distance. I write. Draw. Dream on paper.

Monday. I spent the night with Sara. She lives in Santa Rosa, only a few miles from my temporary quarters in Petaluma. I got on the road early, to return to my room at Ernesto's. The house is cold, clean. It's gray outside, a damp winter morning. I turn on the heater. Select music. Fill the rooms with the sound of Bach's Brandenburg Concertos. Then I prepare my coffee, dark French roast in a ceramic cup, topped with warm, foamy cream, scattered with cinnamon and nutmeg, just for the scent.

I'm reading Hermann Hesse. *Rosshalde*. Like Veraguth, the artist hero who owns the Rosshalde estate, I feel well-ordered, presiding over what is mine, commanding my own estate, this small room edged with windows. This happens when I'm reading Hesse; he permeates the way I live. I decide on my morning: I will tend to bills, to letters, to phone calls, all the necessary details. My time with Sara has left me feeling quiet—in my bones and muscles, in my mind.

I called her late yesterday afternoon, unable to bear any longer the flood of feeling, my heart aching.

"I didn't really leave you when I left you," she said.

It was true. I could sense her everywhere in the house. She asked me to come over and as soon as the invitation came, I was all right. What had been pressing in on me turned to calm, and I delayed leaving for several hours. Work, a bath, a light supper. Then I drove up the highway, in the fog, to Sara.

She had been at her desk, and stopped her work to talk for a while. She noticed me occasionally stretching my neck and asked me about it. The pain in my neck and shoulder had been afflicting me for several days. Slowly, expertly, she massaged the area and took away the pain. I thanked her profusely and she went back to her desk, to write and complete the work for her portfolio.

Sara wants to be a licensed marriage and family therapist, and she's putting in the clinical hours and study required to achieve her goal. I settled on the bed, propped up on pillows, reading Hesse, while she remained bent over the books and paper on her desk.

We stayed like that for the evening. I was glad to be with her, and glad she could write while I was there. Near midnight I went for a walk. It was cold outside, silent. The neighborhood houses were dark. I thought what it would be like to have my own grounds, my own Rosshalde, and I wished for the freedom to write each day, to be like Veraguth, who awakes each morning and turns to his brushes, his easel, his painting.

When I came back, Sara had finished her portfolio. There was still more to do, but at least this much, the written work, was done. I congratulated her, then realized she was nervous because we were going to bed. Sara is conflicted about being with me. Or anyone. She's conflicted about being sexual. She loves me, she wants to be near me, but she isn't sure about the sex.

"It's all right," I told her. "We won't do anything." In bed, we held each other.

"Is it really all right?" she asked.

I smiled at her, laughing a little. "It's all right, Sara. I'm not suffering." But I wanted to kiss her, and to have her kiss me, more than I've wanted anything in a long time.

"We can go slowly," she said.

"Yes, slowly. By degrees."

We were both wide awake, but I was finding it too difficult to lie there next to her and keep passion in check. I told her I had to go to sleep. And as I was closing my eyes, drifting off into the safety of sleep, I heard Sara say my name. I opened my eyes and looked at her.

"Yes," she said, and finally, oh so slowly, her lips parted and I kissed her, a long, lingering kiss. Her kiss was so sweet, like fresh spring water. I drank her, and kept on drinking. We made love, and it was easy and simple and good. Afterwards, I slept.

A deep sleep. No dreams. Memory of Sara, in the midst of our lovemaking, whispering, "You're slower than I am. I knew I wanted you the first time I saw you."

In the morning, Sara is beautiful, radiant, her long dark hair spilling across her shoulders. During all my time with Stephanie, Sara is the only other woman I have been with. Sara and I skirted around each other for a long while, both of us involved with someone else, both of us irresistibly drawn to each other.

For breakfast, Sara feeds me apples and cheese, and toast with butter. She warms yesterday's coffee and pours a cup for me. I take a sip, then put the cup down at a slight distance. I can't drink that bitter dead brew. There isn't enough politeness or love in me to drink yesterday's coffee.

Just that, the coffee, makes me think that nothing can unravel my relationship with Stephanie. Sara is beautiful and I love her. I'm grateful for her friendship. But in all those day-to-day ways that people have, in what they choose to keep around them and in the small things they care about, it is Stephanie who is my mate.

And though we're living apart, and she claims we are free to see and sleep with others, I know—when Stephanie finds out about Sara—she will be jealous.

WHIRLWIND

Ernesto is with his lady at her place, where he spends most of his nights and weekends. I'm alone, reading, when Sara arrives. She's wearing dark tailored slacks, a soft, creamy blouse, a deep–blue velvet tunic. Her eyes are clear, and her thick black hair streaked with gray falls around her face in cascades of energy. As soon as she walks in, the phone rings. I answer, then hold the receiver out to her. "It's for you." Sara looks at me. "Paula," I say.

"I told her I was on my way here."

I return to my book and try not to listen. It's impossible, because Paula is the other woman in Sara's life. Paula claims she doesn't want to be with Sara, or anyone, but she cannot let Sara go. It's disconcerting. And funny.

When that conversation is over, our conversation begins. I tell Sara about feeling pulled away from work, from writing, from Stephanie, from my own sense of independence. "I don't want to feel pulled," I tell her. "I don't want an affair. I don't want to be hung up on you."

"But I do want you to be hung up on me," she answers. "I want you to be involved. I want you to desire me, want to be with me. I want to enter the whirlwind with you, and I want to choose it, out of strength, with eyes open—not from weakness, not pulled in. Do you understand? Walking in because we choose it."

And the writer in me takes a breath, slightly intoxicated by that image—the two of us walking together into a swirling chaos. How can you not get drunk on a woman who looks like this and beckons you into a whirlwind of love?

When we look at each other, there is too much emotion, too much heat. I feel a thin veneer of protection around me, but I know it's dissolving. Rapidly. I will not send her away. After all, she's hungry, and I've cooked dinner for us. We sit down at the kitchen table.

"I'm too nervous to eat," she says.

"All right," I say. "No more melodrama. Don't think about it right now. Us. Anything. Let's eat dinner in peace. Let's pretend we're friends, having an hour together, chatting about our day. I'll put on some music, we'll talk, eat. Pretend there's nothing more than the music, the food, the talk about today."

Instead of today, she asks me about Sunday. I spent it on my own. I drove to Stinson Beach, past fields bathed in sunlight, the hills of Marin rolling gently up to a blue sky. The ocean was clear and bright. As the red sun disappeared into the Pacific, I ran on the wet sand. Ran until I was spent, out of breath. I was on my own, knowing that Stephanie was with Nora, and I felt no trace of jealousy. Reason enough to celebrate.

Sara and I lie down together. For a while, we're quiet, holding each other and listening to the night outside the windows. "I was pulling you all day," Sara tells me. "Pulling. Because I wanted so much to be with you. Every hour that went by, each meeting, I would think, good, that has passed. I am one hour closer to Cristina. All those things today I had to do, they were all steps on the journey to you."

I'm safe. Calm. No chaos, no whirlwind. We sleep. But in the morning, when it's time for her to leave, our lips meet and we kiss, and I'm reeling again. I want the kiss to go on forever, I want our lips, arms, legs, skin, all to melt into each other so that at last, I will be satisfied, I will drink enough and have my fill of Sara.

ADVICE

I tell Sara that my time here at Ernesto's house will soon be over. My days of shuttling between Sonoma County and the city are coming to an end. I have to return to San Francisco. I have a book to finish. I have to work.

"What are you saying?"

"Just that we won't have much time together."

"All right. I won't like it. But I'll accept it. And once I accept it, I'll see that it's perfect. It doesn't mean I won't yearn for you. I do. I yearn, I want to be with you." She strokes my hair. "In February, you'll be gone. And March, April, May. You'll be gone and I'll be longing for you. I'll always long for you, always."

As Sara gathers her clothes, she says, "Advice. Advice for you today, for next week, for always. Be with me when you're with me, even if I'm not physically here. Be with me. If you feel me with you, acknowledge me. Say hello, Sara. Hello. Then you can go on. Don't wince. No wincing. The wincing only prolongs it. Be with me when you're with me."

Excellent advice. I watch her dress, and I'm astonished. Once again, she is well-tailored, yet soft, lovely. Aware of her beauty, but without vanity. "You look good," I say. "Really good."

"I have a lot of beautiful clothes," she says. "You thought I was just country funk, didn't you? You'll see. I'll surprise you."

And she is gone for the day.

NIGHT TALK

In the darkness before dawn, I'm awake, searching for you, wanting to touch you. You turn toward me and say, "I want to marry you forever."

"That's just the night talking," I whisper. And we sink into each other, and begin the day with our lovemaking.

WORDS

December 1974. Friday. So little sleep, and I had to be on the road—heading back to San Francisco—at 6 a.m. My intention is to stay in the city for a few days and focus on turning research notes into sentences and paragraphs worth reading. By the time I cross the Golden Gate Bridge, I'm tired. I stop at Malvina's in North Beach, and try to punch myself awake with two cappuccinos. Ridiculous. When I arrive at my studio apartment on Gladys Street, I'm ragged, edgy.

The hours go by. The speed in my system begins to dissipate, and I settle down to write. The phone rings. It's Carolyn, the one person I didn't want to talk to, but I know I must. It's been weeks since I've seen her. Our occasional phone conversations have left me cautious, wary of spending time with her. Part of me is always guarding myself against her mood swings. When we last spoke, we had decided to see a play together, but I ended up begging off. Now we have the conversation I've been avoiding. She wants to know my real reason for bailing out on the theatre trip we had planned. Did it have anything to do with her? Yes.

"I didn't like the roles we were getting into," I tell her. "It felt old."

"What roles?"

"Me being perfect and centered," I say, "and you being flipped out and fucked up." I tell her that I don't have time for mind games. I remind her that I'm trying to finish a book.

She gets angry. "You're being precious."

"What does that mean?"

"Precious about your writing."

I grit my teeth, trying to control my resentment at her description of me. This is what happens with Carolyn, what used to happen when we lived together. No matter where we started, I'd feel goaded into a completely irrational version of myself. I close my eyes, take a deep breath. "I'm not being precious."

"What do you call it then?"

"Damn it, Carolyn!" I pause, trying again for control, but the anger is still there, in my voice. *"I'm-meeting-a-deadline."*

She takes a different tack. She knows about deadlines; she knows how disciplined I am. She reminds me that she has always believed in me. For a while, I go along with her. This was our original bond, two artists struggling to do our best work, both of us with a deep desire to be true to our calling. We could always share whatever we were working on, and count on each other for honest feedback. That was when we were equals, before our relationship fell apart. Before it became a one-up, one-down version of what used to be. It doesn't take long for her to start in again about the way it was, the way we were in better times. She recalls the person I was then—the friend she admired, the lover I once was.

"Stop it," I say. "Please. Stop."

"Stop what?"

"Get me off the damn altar!" I lower my voice. "I'm not the greatest lover you ever had. I'm not the best friend in the world. I blow it sometimes. I don't live up to my commitments. I walk out."

We keep at it. After a while, against all odds, we work it out. Finally, we're laughing, and we say goodbye. I hang up, then remain motionless for a few minutes. Somewhere inside me, I feel a thread snap. I remember how it was with Carolyn, how intensely we loved each other. Now we lead separate lives.

It seems to be moving in the same direction with Stephanie, who spends more and more time with Nora. Though Stephanie says she can't live without me, the day may come when she'll feel differently. She may want to stay with Nora. Or she'll find another lover, and fall in love with her; she'll be happy with someone else.

I think of friends who would probably agree that I don't always live up to my commitments. I do blow it now and then. And one of these days, Sara may wake up and snap out of her love trance. I don't want to be with you, she'll say. And she'll walk out.

Suddenly, I feel ridiculous. Insignificant. Like a beer can you throw away. Never mind. I go to my desk, roll paper into the carriage of the typewriter. The words in my mind, in my heart, ask nothing of me, except to come through me onto the page. Maybe everyone will leave. I still have words. I can carve a life out of my typewriter.

WE NEVER MEAN TO FALL IN LOVE

As I'm drifting into gloom, smoking a Sherman, drinking black coffee and thoroughly immersing myself in the mood of *Rosshalde*, I get a call from Renée. Renée and her husband Daniel came into my life through Stephanie, who has known them for a long time. Soon after Stephanie and I became a couple, they invited us to dinner. We were friends from our first hour together. Renée and Daniel live in a beautiful house on a San Francisco hillside. I felt instantly at home there. I was drawn to the vibrant color in their surroundings, their taste in art and decor, their love of books and film, fine wine and good food. They have money and spend it well. Perhaps by that I mean they spend their money in ways that make sense to me.

Renée tells me that she and Daniel are on their way to a wine-tasting, and she invites me to join them. I accept. Somehow the evening doesn't hold quite the same magic I've so often experienced with them, with their *joie de vivre* that is infectious. Perhaps I've brought some of my own gloom with me. The faces around the room look blank, not quite present. I content myself with Daniel's laughter, and the geniality of our host, Jon. I love the warmth of Jon's voice as he talks about Liebfraumilch and Chenin Blanc. Most of all, I enjoy listening to Renée and Daniel, hearing them recount their day, a day that began with breakfast at the Belgian Waffle. They tell us in detail how delicious it was.

Their anecdotes remind me of my desire to be rich and famous. Now it doesn't seem important to be famous. I just want to be rich. Rich enough to stop in at the Bottle Shop in Sausalito and buy a good bottle of Liebfraumilch for Stephanie's solar eclipse birthday. Rich enough to take all my friends to breakfast at the Belgian Waffle, and to include everyone for tempura dinner on a Friday evening. There's so much sweetness to life and I want to taste it all, to shower my friends with gifts, with love, to indulge their whims.

At home again after the wine-tasting, a call from Stephanie. She needs to see me. Tomorrow evening, she says. She must see me. I'm certain she wants to talk about Sara.

We never mean to fall in love. It was not my intent. I'm back again at Ernesto's house, where I look past the avocado leaves to the yellow roses blooming outside, beyond the aging white-washed fence of our neighbors, out to a sky heavy with mist and fog. It's cold in the house, difficult to work. I feel soft, full. This morning, Sara said, "I feel so fortunate to be around you."

Last night, I told her, "I'm in love with everyone. With life, with the universe."

"I'm glad," she said. "I feel easier with someone who loves more than me."

I'm in love with you, Sara. As we lie together in bed, I hold my hand against your belly, sending warmth into your center. We stay there, listening to the morning, listening to music, and in the heart of listening, I say silently, I love you, I love you. When you look at me, your eyes are full of light, and I have to turn away. Now there is all this feeling in me.

This is for all of us who are in love with more than one, grappling with the rule that was given us: one and only one. But I am wedded to the whole earth—how can I love just one?

Late September, 2010. Friday afternoon. I listen to the mournful cello of Yo-Yo Ma and look out at a blue sky, white clouds drifting in from the west. The trees that grace the green span of lawn behind the house have already begun to take on their autumn color. The hillock outside my studio window is carpeted with moss, and the leaves of the rhododendron bushes are turning yellow. I watch leaves fall from the branch and drift to the ground.

As I gaze out at this day from a comfortable space, surrounded by my books, photographs, and cherished objects, I find I am still wedded to the whole earth, still in love with her grand panoramas and infinitesimal miracles. Though I'm no longer in love with two women, my memories of that other era are stirred by the music of Elgar's Cello Concerto, opulent and romantic. I listen to the music, and reflect on the times I've lived through.

In the '70s, when I was dealing with the highs and lows of two women in my life, we were a liberated lot. Our liberation began in the decade that threw off the tight-bind, tight-mind restrictions of the '50s. We elected John F. Kennedy to the White House in 1960, and while he was there, America's youth stepped forward and declared a new day. Everything seemed possible. Reaching for the moon was no longer wishful thinking—it was an imperative.

When JFK was gunned down, the darkness at first overwhelmed us and then, like a shadowed fog, it crept in all around us. There was Vietnam and the struggle for civil rights, and the horrific clashes brought on by both conflicts. We lost singular lives in the civil rights movement, thousands in Vietnam. Before the decade was over, ignorance and hatred crushed us again: we lost Martin Luther King, Jr. and Robert Kennedy. The grief seemed unending.

Through all that turmoil, we had sex, drugs, rock and roll. By the '70s, sex was no longer a subtle innuendo; it was up front and center in our music and movies, in advertising, in our lives. It was blatant and pervasive. Women had the pill and if one were inclined to be promiscuous, promiscuity was safer than it had ever been before. Feminism was coming into its own and women were rebelling against their assigned roles. Gay people were coming out of the closet and taking on a new identity. Open marriages and open relationships were a part of the social parlance.

All of that was going on around me in the wider society, but I wasn't thinking about society as a whole. I only knew what was going on in my own corner of the world. I lived in Northern California, in San Francisco and Sonoma County. In that part of the world, and amongst the people I generally associated with, it was okay for me to love a woman, and it was okay for me to sleep with, and love, more than one woman. What was not okay, in my own mind, was for me to be jealous of my lovers seeing other people. The two women in my life were using the same playbook. They knew it wasn't okay for them to be jealous of me shuttling between them. We were trying to create a new paradigm, one that defied the parameters we had been given by our parents.

The new paradigm worked well for sexual escapades. It was only problematic when emotions became a part of the equation—when, without meaning to, we fell in love. Now, as I read the journals I kept during those years, I find that my struggle with jealousy is a recurring theme. When I was a virgin Catholic, I wanted to be pure of heart, body, and mind. As a young adult, I aspired to a new standard of purity. I wanted to be the kind of person who was beyond the experience of jealousy, a person free of the inner demand to say—and feel—she is mine, and mine alone. I wanted love cleansed of jealousy. I even thought of it in those terms, as if jealousy were an emotion that could be scrubbed away. For brief periods of time, I believed I had attained the emotional freedom required by the standard-bearers of open relationships, but it was an illusion—a transitory state I could not make permanent.

When I look back, I see I was not only grappling with the confusion and negative emotions that were a consequence of being seriously involved with two people. I had also deluded myself into thinking that I hadn't meant to fall in love. All those years ago, I was a romantic. I still am. The romantic in me walks hand in hand with the realist, and the realist knows that love doesn't always pan out, or last. The realist also knows that our individual stories are played out in a much larger context, one that is complex and challenging. I am ever aware that we have big problems to solve. I can see the stark underbelly of this world, where so many are impoverished and imprisoned. I want with all my heart to see us overcome those problems, to find solutions and create a world where all of us can, if we wish, enjoy the occasional sweetness of a romantic's vision. Even when that goal seems nearly impossible to attain, I choose to believe. I believe in love, believe in its power to inspire and sustain us, heal and confound us, root us in time and place, and carry us to mysterious and unimaginable frontiers.

In saying I believe in love, I mean something beyond romantic love. When we find someone with whom we can be completely genuine, someone who affirms our sense of authenticity, we want to stay connected to that person. Most of us search for someone who understands our concerns and values, a person with whom we can share our life. Our inner compass is naturally directed to true communion, to a place where we can settle and take root. We want to say, and feel, *yes:* This is where I belong.

Now, after all these years, I understand that search. I understand myself. The truth is, I always meant to fall in love, I always meant to find love. That's what it was all about. Whenever I felt the possibility of something more than an adventure or an affair, my heart and mind would follow my body, and I let myself believe that this was it.

Along the way, I broke some hearts and had my own heart broken. After each unraveling, the regret and disappointment would make me wary for a time. But then my heart would recover, and the quest would continue. During those years when I was attempting to discover where I belonged, what to do, where to be and who to be with, all the while that I was falling in and out of love, I had a singular and compelling need fueling my journey through the world. I believed, deep down, there was one person I was meant to be with—one person I would fall in love with, who would fall in love with me. I believed we would stay together and love each other for a lifetime. I wanted to claim and be claimed. I was looking for the love of my life.

SOLSTICE

December 1974. Roll back the days. Roll back to Stevie Wonder singing, *"Here we are on earth together ... you and I ... God has made us fall in love ..."* I remember being close to Sara, moving slowly, dancing to this music. My heart fills and spills into prayer. I want to love like this always and never cause pain.

Solstice. The day begins gray and wet and heavy. The rain spills down, and I awake with Sara. This is our last morning together. Not forever, but it seems like forever. For innumerable reasons, we must part. It will be a long time before Sara and I see each other again.

On the eve of Solstice, in the dark, in bed together, I hear Sara say, "Well, since this is our last night..."

"Yes?"

"Let's get it on."

"Are you sure?"

"No. I'm nervous. I probably can't do it."

For a while, I'm quiet, lying still beside her. Sara matches my stillness, then breaks the silence.

"What?"

"I know what I'll do." I pause. "I'll make you wait. I'll make you wait, and wait, and wait…"

She smiles. "And then?"

"Then … I'll make you wait some more. Wait, Sara, wait …" I caress her soft skin, gently, gently. She knows I cannot wait. We move together, cling to one another, lose ourselves in loving, in sex, in pleasure. We rise and fall and rise again to that ecstatic height that belongs to lovers, and then we rest in the warmth that envelops us and sends us into sleep.

When I leave her in the morning to begin my day, I have a plan, and I'm determined to stay with the plan. I will see Sara for a little while in the afternoon. An hour or two more with her, I tell myself. That's all. Having settled that in my mind, I drive in the fog to a morning seminar. Everyone in the room seems so easy, so relaxed. The sun comes out and it shines bright and warm on the winter green fields of Sonoma. All I want is to be with Sara. Forget the plan. The day is too sweet.

I leave the seminar early and go to Sara's house. She feeds me onion soup. It's delicious. Then she brews a pot of fresh coffee. She understands now how much I love good coffee, and she serves me a cup of dark roast topped with foamy cream. Good. Much too good. I'm not used to being in her space, letting her take care of me.

Mid-afternoon. Gabrielle arrives. She's from Germany. She's tall, big-boned, heavy, with dark hair and deep-brown eyes. Gabrielle is here to study psychology. She opens her tapestry bag and says, "I have all kinds of cigarettes. All kinds. What do you want? Cigarettes from India, cigarettes scented with clove, gold-wrapped cigarettes." And then she produces a bottle of Chianti, wrapped in straw. Gabrielle is full of mystery and secrets. Secrets that I will probably never know. I like her.

We all go together to Imwalle's and shop for organic vegetables. Sara hugs me and thanks me for introducing her to this big roadside stand filled with fruits and vegetables. Mike, who owns Imwalle's, hugs me because it's Christmas, and because he's an old Italian who loves to flirt. On the way back to Sara's, we stop and play Frisbee in the park. I must go home, I tell her. I must. Sara insists on making me coffee before I go. I accept.

Gabrielle and I get stoned while Sara makes coffee in the kitchen. We put a record on, Buffalo Springfield. I'm dancing, getting high, really high. Then the music changes and it's Stevie Wonder singing, "... *you are the sunshine of my life.*" Why do certain songs become "our song" when we're in love? This is our song now—it belongs to Sara and me. She dances with me and that's it. It's all over for me. She can move, Jesus, sweet Jesus, she moves incredibly. I've found her. My lifetime dance partner. We dance, dance, dance, until we collapse.

Gabrielle looks at her watch. "Pretty good," she declares. "Four minutes and fifty-five seconds."

I laugh. Eternity in four minutes and fifty-five seconds.

We drink coffee, talk, quiet down. Sara brings out her clarinet and plays for us. She is wonderful. Her music, beautiful. When she's finished, she looks at us and smiles. "God came through," she says. Yes.

I return to Ernesto's, who is gone for the holidays. I put some order to my room and our common living areas. Change my clothes. Put on music. Dance. It's solstice, and I can't stop dancing. Gabrielle and Sara arrive. Because we're reluctant to face that long stretch of time before we can be together again, Sara and I are squeezing in as many visits as we can. We exchange Christmas presents. Without asking or thinking or knowing, we have given each other bracelets. Mine to her is delicate, light. Black macramé inlaid with deep-red stones. They remind me of the dark passion beneath the quiet of her reserve. Beneath the reticence, a promise. The bracelet she gives me is heavy, a wide copper band with a triangular symbol. For the Scorpio, the Indian.

Sara and Gabrielle are going to a party. That isn't what I want to do. They try to persuade me, then at last, they go on without me. But as it nears eleven, I think it's time to leave the peace and quiet of my home. Time to face the unknown. I decide to go to the party. Sara will be there, so no matter what, it's bound to be good.

I drive up the highway to Santa Rosa, to a big woodframe house. All the lights are on, lots of cars around. I walk into the house and the music is on, the party is on. I see Sara and know I have lost my heart completely. Yesterday, perhaps even this morning, I had an ounce of protection, a thin screen of safety. It's all gone.

Sara is wearing a print blouse that clings to the curve of her breasts, and soft fabric pants that look like a skirt.

The material moves with her, and I cannot take my eyes from her. She is the essence of womanliness. Watching her, a kind of sweet madness wells up in me. The way she moves, the rhythm and flow, the exquisite beauty that is Sara dancing, sweeps away all reason and logic. This afternoon, she said to me, whatever it is you've got, I want it. I want it.

Now you have it, Sara. You have it all. I'm in love with you and there is no turning back. I surrender to Solstice.

TRESPASS

Christmas Eve. There are presents beneath the tree. My home on Gladys Street pleases me. Everywhere I look, it's clean, warm. Memory of Stephanie lying with me at twilight, the sound of her pleasure. "Two years," she says. "Two years it took us to get here. I'm not giving this up. You're not leaving me, ever. Forget it." She turns to the window. "Look at the sky," she says. I look. The sky is orange and pink and twilight blue. "We did that," Stephanie says. "That sky. We did that with our loving."

Our love, like the light, is all over the house.

Sonoma winter in the sun. Green hills and the gray bark of the trees. December orchards. Stephanie and I pick persimmons from a tree in an orchard where a sign is posted: No Trespassing. We trespass all over it and then sit for a while by a pine tree, drinking Barbera wine and eating tangerines, watching the sun settle behind the hills and into the ocean. Life is good.

When I return home, I call Sara. "You have two women in love with you," she says. "Two."

I know. I know.

FALL INTO INFINITY

The time apart from Sara is over. I'm in my room at Ernesto's house, waiting for Sara to arrive. I become aware of a subtle uneasiness, a new sensation. For the first time in my life, I don't like being in love. I've always welcomed this enchanted state with open arms, like an old friend. But now the sense of needing someone else is uncomfortable. I dislike the loss of my independence, the simple enjoyment I felt in being by myself. Barely a week ago, I was content with time alone. If I was unhappy or angry about something, it had only to do with myself.

Now, today, I find I'm dejected because Sara left a note here while I was out. The note says she can't see me until after ten tonight. I'm disappointed. I had expected her to be here by early evening. Losing that handful of hours with her has made me sad all day.

I find this state of mind absurd. I take a walk to change my mood, then settle down to read Hesse. His writing helps me reconnect with the energy of the artist, the clean demands of discipline. Coffee, a smoke, music. The way through to Sara's arrival at my door.

A strange light today. Fog rolling in from the ocean in the late afternoon, with the winter sun breaking through the misty air. It was a dream-like world that I drifted through, like a sleepwalker.

I'm wondering what I need of Sara. It isn't sex. We haven't known each other long enough, and there is still her uncertainty. With Stephanie, there's no uncertainty. There's a richness to loving Stephanie, a richness that flows into our meals together, the music we make, the way we can laugh and be silly. We are happy hedonists. Isn't that enough? It is. More than enough. What, then, do I need of Sara? The light in her eyes when she looks at me? Good God, that seems so romantic and useless.

I have the urge to say no to Sara. No, you cannot see me at ten. Better to end this now, while I'm feeling how uncomfortable all this is, how it confuses the perfect clarity I felt only last week. I stand by the heater, puffing on a cigarette, ignoring the fact that it's beginning to give me a headache. I'm asking myself a question. Would I actually turn away love? How unlike me. And yet there is a voice in my head saying, yes, why not? Refuse love. For once in your life, refuse. Doesn't it make sense to say no to her? What, after all, can I offer her?

Sara and I want different things in life. She loves the country; I want the city. Soon I'll be back in San Francisco, and I sense that it's time for me to return to my roots in theatre, the first place where I felt kinship out in the world, the joy of working and playing with a group of people who became my friends, and then, a new kind of family. If I pursue that life again, it will place Sara and me in separate worlds, and put even more miles between us. It troubles me to think that I will establish myself in the city, and still be tied to Sonoma, to Sara. In the end, what can we give each other? I'll never be her mate. We're not right for each other. Though Stephanie and I live apart, I feel married to her in a way that I will never be to Sara.

What do we have, Sara and I? A few nights out of the month. Here and there, a whole day together. Is the feeling of her arms around me at night enough to call me away from the life I want, the work I want? I don't like this confusion, this impatience for the phone to ring, waiting for the hours to pass until I can be with her again. I don't want to be somewhere else in my mind while I'm walking along a street with Stephanie. All of that seems wrong—a denial of my life and the awareness of what *is*, moment to moment. For the first time, I feel love as agitation, discomfort, a slight fever that distorts my sensibility.

Even as I build this case against becoming involved, it's difficult to imagine actually refusing to see Sara, refusing another night with her. I must at least talk to her.

At first, we were friends. The friendship was good, it made me feel strong. The affair is not to my liking. I sigh, smile, crush my cigarette into an ashtray. As I return to my desk, I catch a glimpse of myself in the mirror. The woman there in the glass has just turned thirty-three, and she's considering the possibility of making unfamiliar choices. Will she turn away love? Really? We will wait and see how the next chapter unfolds.

At nine o'clock the phone rings. It's Sara, wanting to know if she should come over.

"I don't know." Long silence. "I had a strange day," I tell her. "I asked myself a lot of questions about us. I don't know if it's right." Another long silence.

"And?"

"I've been miserable all day and I didn't like it."

"Yes. I understand."

Why? Why does she understand? "I'm wondering if we shouldn't just end this now." Then I say, "And I don't know if I can end it if I see you."

"I know," she says. "It's harder if we see each other." There's a pause. "Maybe I shouldn't come over."

No. Wait. I don't want to hear that. Do I? "We have to talk at some point," I tell her. "I can't just ..." I don't know how to finish my sentence. I take a breath. "I don't want to do this on the phone. The phone is insane."

"So, I should come over. Is that what you're saying?"

"I'm afraid if I see you—it feels like falling into an abyss."

"Whatever we do," Sara says, "we have to do it with our eyes open. That's what I want. To have our eyes open, to be aware." Sara's voice is quiet, clear. "If I come over tonight, if we see each other, then we're agreeing to fall into the abyss together, tonight."

Her voice pulls me down, down. I begin to want the fall.

"Or we could just say goodbye," I say. "Now, on the phone."

"We could, yes." Again, there's a pause. "I think I can do that," she says.

Silence. I wait.

"It feels like being an alcoholic in a cheap hotel room, with not much liquor left in the bottle. Dry. Really dry. But we could do that."

The image captures me. A painting by Edward Hopper on a back-alley wall. Her description fits. It's true. And much too depressing. I breathe in.

"You're right," I say. "Just come over. I have to see you. We have to talk."

"Shall I call again, just to be sure?"

"No. Yes. Maybe."

"I want you to know I'm dying to see you. I don't have to come if you don't want me to, but I've been wanting to be with you all day."

"And I was miserable because I had to wait three more hours to see you. It's crazy. I don't like it."

In the end, we agree that we don't need any more phone calls. "Just come," I tell her. I go outside, walk in the fog along my quiet street, pluck a pink rose. What are our alternatives? Can we work out a relationship that doesn't cost us pain? That doesn't drain us? I don't know.

Underneath it all, my sense of humor is irrepressible. Just beneath the questions, the doubts—laughter.

It doesn't take long to see that I'm laughing at myself. Through this whole day and most of the evening, I've been thinking, thinking, thinking. Weighing pros and cons, arguing with myself over whether to continue this relationship. When Sara arrives, when I see her, my brain comes to a standstill. All I want to do is gather her in, take her to bed, make love to her. Only an hour ago, when I was alone in this room, my objections to our affair were clear and defined. Now they are clouded, weak. But I'm not the only one with doubts about the relationship. Sara is also struggling with whether to continue, asking herself if we can find a way forward, asking if we should even try.

We talk for a while, our voices low, full of love and the confusion our love has caused. Gradually, there are fewer and fewer words. I know I want her. I can see and feel that she wants me. Her desire is palpable and real. Knowing this, feeling her pull me toward her, stirs a faint memory of a moment in the film *Zorba the Greek,* when the young man played by Alan Bates turns away the tremulous and radiant Irene Papas. *You fool,* I thought to myself. I don't want to be that fool.

I wake in the night and listen to the wind and the spattering of rain on the window. Sara is close beside me, deep in sleep. Our bodies are warm, heavy with love, with sex spent as if there were no tomorrow. Perhaps because that was a possibility. We knew that one of us, perhaps both of us, might choose to end it.

I breathe, and listen to the earth sighing, singing rain. I remember that moment, only hours ago, when I stood poised at the edge of a question: Would I turn away love?

Sara and I, circling that question, two beautiful beings hovering in the velvet sky, flashing our wings in the starlight, looking down into the abyss. There, far below us, are the glistening curves of a river, a river rolling slowly through a deep womb of earth. The water becomes a thousand strands of light, and in that liquid light, we know there is a promise. In the abyss, in the dark matrix of mother earth, there is the sweetest water in the universe.

We move toward one another, closer and closer, and the question dissolves. We embrace and let ourselves fall. Down, down, down. The water is there, in the resplendent abyss. We have to drink.

I am doing all that I can. I am describing this fall into infinity. We love, we fight, we give pleasure and pain. We cry, we soothe, turn away, turn back. We surrender.

We are drinking from that mythical cup, quenching our thirst to be part of, close to, one with, quenching our need for union. We are listening to one another, telling our tales and extravagant fables. We are living the love stories told through all the centuries.

Sara's Prayer

It rained all through the night. The morning is warm, the air is wet and clean. Outside, the trees are glistening. A bird sings. Traces of fog drift above the hills in the distance. Sara had to return to her house to change, pick up things she needed for today, so I offered to drive her. Afterwards, I'll take her back to her car. It gives us a little more time together.

I'm sitting in Sara's kitchen, watching her. Her face is lifted upward, her eyes are closed. She's praying.

"Dear God, please help me today not to be a fool. Please, dear God, help me get it together out there. I can only be like this with you, with my friends, with Cristina. Out there, I can't be a fool, so please help me, because it's all you, everything depends on you. I don't want to end up in a mental institution, so please, dear God, help me."

She leaves the kitchen and I look at the picture that Sara keeps on the wall above the dish drain. It's a black-and-white photograph of the holy man Sawan Singh.

I've seen it before, now I really look at it. I see the smile hovering at the edges of his mouth, the bliss, the light that radiates from his eyes. I see him alive in the photograph, pulling me into his ocean of God.

I suddenly want this photograph. I want to look at it every day and meditate on this face and let myself drown in the calm and perfect peace shining from the eyes of Sawan Singh. I hear him calling me and I yell at him silently in my head: yes, yes, I see you. I see you are with God, and yes, I love you and I love God, but you cannot have me, Sawan Singh. I will not give up the world. Even if I embrace you, I will have and hold onto my life in the world. My energy is fierce. I want to swallow the cosmos, to crush everything between these powerful arms.

WORKING IT OUT

The days go by, and the nights. I have a dream of wandering through unlit rooms where crimes have been committed. Even though I try to subdue my fear, those dark rooms cause me to tremble. I thread my way around obstacles, back to a little room where I'm all alone. I awaken feeling lost.

I need time with Stephanie. I go to her and tell her about the conflict I feel between her and Sara. I'm settled in the life Stephanie and I have made together, while at the same time, I'm drawn to Sara and the way she talks of another life, a life with her, north of Sonoma, in Ukiah County. When she's completed her graduate work and all the licensing requirements, she wants to go back to her rural roots. She wants to go back to a small-town life, back to farms, pastures, and vineyards. That's where she feels at home. And she wants me to go with her.

"Are you writing this?" Stephanie asks. "This is important. This is how you work it out."

How do you work it out when two women are in love with you, and you with them?

Stephanie and I make love. It's sweet, perfect. I hold her and kiss her and she cries. As we lie there together, I think about yesterday afternoon. We drove in her van up into the hills and parked beside the road, at a spot looking out over the valley. Sitting in the warm sun on the hillside, we let our thoughts, and our talk, ramble.

Stephanie talked about Nora, who is innocent and wondering, following Stephanie's lead, letting herself be courted. I spoke of Sara, who is asking if we will someday share a house in Hopland.

I realized it isn't only me—all of us are trying to work this out.

"We can dissolve the contract now," Stephanie said. "And if we do, no matter what we say, we'll drift apart and lose each other."

"Here we are, talking about our contract, all logic and reason. How do you feel about me?" I asked her. "What does your heart say? Can you live without me?"

"No."

Now we know where we are, dear Stephanie. Because the truth is I cannot live without you either. I'm willing to dissolve our contract. I am not willing to dissolve our union.

BANSHEE

It's over between Sara and me. We're done. Her banshee demon energy finally wore me out. One whole day, one long night, everything falling apart. Sara turning in circles, rap-rap-rapping about her inadequacy and imperfection and the ways she has failed. She isn't all right, she isn't enlightened. On and on. I try to talk to her, try to make sense of this dissolution, this stream-of-consciousness outpouring. At dawn, we're still awake and she's telling me this is wrong and it isn't good to be with women and somewhere out there is her real mate who is a man and oh, my god, I explode. She has robbed us, taken the holiness from our loving. She has let herself submit to the distortion, the mind-bend, the terrible lies that become ropes—ropes that twist us into a misshapen, shallow semblance of what we were, what we are—rough, heavy cords that cut and bind and knot, a merciless punishment that only stops when we are sufficiently bent to fit society's mold and religion's cross.

Then, for a while, I'm quiet, because I remember. As I look at Sara struggling with the voices in her head, I remember that I was there for so many years—exactly where she is now. Then the moment of understanding passes, and the quiet becomes our voices once again raised against each other, against ourselves. We yell and pound at each other with our words until, at last, I'm worn out and there is nothing more to say and there is no resolution. The fog above the hills clears and Sara is no longer only beautiful, she is also the banshee wailing at the door. She is a woman driven by guilt to condemn and attack—a fierce opponent who has broken me into little pieces and left me utterly exhausted.

It's over. I return to Stephanie, to absorb the peacefulness of her cottage. She feeds me beautiful food and we sit by the firelight and play our guitars and sing. Then she leaves me and saunters into the night, promising to return in a while. I stay by the fire and listen to a violin concerto, resting my eyes, my mind, my soul. The music soothes my spirit, helping me to recover from the all-night-all-day battle with the cosmos and Sara's banshee. I slip into bed, into silence, and then Stephanie is beside me and we sleep. There is no pulling, no tugging, no restlessness, no fear. There is only sleep and trust and our love for each other. I thank God for Stephanie, who heals me.

Stephanie grew up without religion. No church services or reading the Bible. No one to tell her about heaven and hell and how to delineate sin, no one to tell her that she came into this world already imperfect, marked by original sin. Stephanie had a guitar that she held to her breast, vibrating harmony into her heart and sound into her soul. She fell in with a bunch of musicians who made music and sang and laughed; that was her church. She saved enough money to go to Europe and there, she walked and rambled to her heart's content, letting her instincts be her guide. It was in Europe that she discovered splendid food and great coffee. Her pleasure in fine cuisine became her religion; the ritual of preparing food and sharing it with friends became her communion.

When she first fell in love, it was with an older woman who was straight, a woman who drew a strict perimeter around her body. She enjoyed Stephanie's adoration, but stated firmly that theirs was a loving friendship, nothing more. Still, there was no moralizing voice in Stephanie's head, no inner sermon to shame her into denying her feelings. The company of a beautiful woman she adored made the food more delicious, the wine sweeter, the coffee more fragrant. Then I came along and took her to bed, and women became her vocation.

SIX-FIFTHS

Sara calls and asks me to come see her. We talk quietly for a long time and make our peace. I thought we were done, but the love is still there. With all the complications, we still need each other, want each other. Accept what is, Sara says. Yes. We find our way into each other's arms, and all the complications disappear.

The next morning, bright sunshine floods Sara's kitchen, and I am washed in light. Announcement to the kitchen walls: I finally have enough love. All these years, my quest was for love, and at last, I have found the cup I was seeking. I drank deep and I have been filled. My thirst is quenched.

"What we have is perfect," Sara says. "It's perfect that I only have part of you. A third of you. One-third for Stephanie, one-third for you. No. That's not it. Fourths. One-fourth for me. One-fourth for Stephanie. Two-fourths for you. No. Not fourths. Fifths. One-fifth for me. Two-fifths for Stephanie. Three-fifths for you. That's six-fifths. Right. That's right. Six-fifths."

It is right. The invisible spirit of God is the sixth-fifth. Six-fifths I am.

I AM THE MOST BLESSED OF BEINGS

"I am the most blessed of beings on earth," Sara says. She looks at me. "It has something to do with you."

"Do you think so?"

"Yes. Yes. Because you give. Because you love. Because you're patient."

I'm not sure how it happened. These last few days, everything has felt simple, easy. Sara is peaceful, Stephanie is no longer jealous. I was out at sea, tossed by the wind and waves, and now I have washed ashore to an unfamiliar island, a place where barriers have dissolved and the air is sweet. These are halcyon days.

I tell Sara that Stephanie is content. She thinks Sara is a fine, fine lady. Stephanie's words, exactly.

As I leave, Sara calls out to me. "Give her my love," she says. Then she changes her mind. "No. I don't want to say that." She waves good-bye and adds, "Just love her. Love her."

If Truffaut were a woman, she might be filming this story—*Jules et Jim* re-imagined, with a new triangle of lovers. The title would be *Sara et Stephanie,* with me between them. Maybe this time, the story will not end tragically. Maybe. Moment to moment. Lightly, lovingly. Don't hold on.

And in this way, moment to moment, we carry on, trying to suffuse the conflict that has been there from the beginning between Sara and me. Part of her wanted simply to be alone, to be celibate. And that pull to celibacy also evoked an inner judge that told her she should be with a man. For my part, I wanted to love without feeling pain or causing pain. It was impossible. Stephanie's flirtations with other women hurt me, but our relationship felt like home, and I kept returning to the comfort I felt with her. Inevitably, that hurt Sara.

We all tried to fit easily into the sexual liberation our era had provided, but our emotions were measured for more primal attire.

I leave Stephanie at daybreak and go to Sara. It's cold in her house. We only want to hold each other. We lie together with all our clothes on, wrapped in a blanket, talking. Our final hours slip by. Sara puts a record on—*Sonic Seasonings.* She comes back to me and I wrap my arms around her and the ocean sounds wash over us. I want to be inside her. We strip and I move slowly, lightly, hovering over Sara, barely touching her. I wash her skin with my hair and caress her with my hands, my mouth, with the ocean of love I feel for her. Our bodies meld and we slip into that ecstasy where we began, where we forget the world and words and time. When the music stops, we stop. We hold each other. My love. My love.

After that winter day with Sara, I went back to San Francisco. My work at the college was finished, and I moved my few belongings from my temporary place in Ernesto's home. Sara and I each went to our individual concerns and obligations, our separate lives. There are no more pages recording the tumult of my affair with her. There is only a letter from Sara: *I have given a lot of thought to our relationship, to us, and realized that I have a deeper desire for commitment and involvement with you than you have for me. This is a painful situation for me. And so, I think—I wish to take a break from being with you for a while.*

There was no note of finality; she ended the letter by saying she was open to meeting with me to discuss this, if I wanted. I remember the ache I felt, the desire to be with her, and the certain sense that if we did meet, our feeling for one another would carry us again into a world of pain. Sara and I were too much alike: much too intense, and both of us God-hungry. She sometimes chided me for being too egoistic, and once had become furious with me, yelling at the top of her lungs, "You're not the main one! God is the main one, not you! God is the main one."

October 2010. Tuesday afternoon. When I think back to Sara yelling at me that day, I can only conclude she was right: I was full of myself. But I know now that the self-involved, much-loved only child in me had kept me safe from permanent exile. Had it not been for that part of myself, I stood a good chance of being cast into a spiritual desert. Secure in my mother's love and in God's love, I was able to stand up to a religion that condemned homosexuals, demanding that we re-make ourselves into a lie that would be worthy of the Church's blessing. My ego may have blinded me to certain things—and made me a pain to live with at times—but I'm grateful now that my ego was strong enough to hold against the weight of judgment that pressed down against my sense of self. Religion had a scepter at my back, but could not break my spine. Society had its boot at my throat, but could not force me to stay silent, closeted away, out of sight.

And though I'm glad of anything and everything that helped me survive being assailed by society and the Church, I also understood what Sara was saying when she insisted that God was the main one, not me. Once in a while, long after we had parted, I recalled her voice and I would mentally hold out my hand to quiet my ego: step back, I would think to myself. Step aside. Those were the moments when I remembered that each one of us is the main character in our own story, and that there is always a larger story that encompasses all of us. The Church would not bless me, but Sara's love, and her honesty, did.

SAVED BY THE NET

I have been traveling between the present and the past in this memoir, skipping back and forth and back again, writing the story of my unfolding in the only way that made sense to me. It is easy to say we are born, we live, we die. But the emotional sense of that middle part cannot be written about in an orderly, chronological way—at least, not by me.

Reading over what I have written has led me to reflect on what remains unwritten, those periods of time I've not included in these pages. The decision to lay aside certain memories means there are people left out—family, friends, lovers.

I set out in this work to remember and write about women I have loved, and to record my pathway through the forces locked in opposition to that love. In light of that endeavor, I must note that there are four years missing between the mid-winter when Sara and I parted and the summer when I left Northern California to move to Los Angeles.

Sex and Soul Redux

I fell in love twice during those four years. There was a brief, impossible, incredibly intense romance with a writer who kept faith with her journal; she went on to become a truly fine poet. A year and some months after that affair ended, I began a relationship with a woman who was a therapist and a mother; we lived together for nearly two years. We both wanted it to take, but she was rooted in her home and in her children, and I was called to the road. It wasn't that simple, but these things never are.

Both these women were an integral part of my path to salvation. All those who love us, I believe, form the net that saves us from the depths—the depths we stumble into, innocent, unaware; and the depths we wade or jump into, confident that we know what we're doing. Thank God, thank goodness, for the people who love us.

As for the years left out of this memoir—with the love and the pain, the discoveries, decisions and revelations they hold—I have not and cannot write about them here, for reasons that both the heart, and art, dictate.

THE MORAL ARC

October 2010. Wednesday morning. It's a perfect autumn day: bright sun, cool air. The subtle sting of winter's chill is beginning its slow burn of the leafy trees. As I contemplate the hours before me, I find myself grappling with a way to express a shift in perception that is directly linked to writing this memoir. Over the course of the past year, I have been following the current of memory and now, I have come ashore in unexpected territory. What began as a personal story soon blended with my spiritual journey, and that blending has led me to understand that both the story and the journey are intertwined with politics.

The span of years recounted in these pages was a time of sexual awakening and discovery. It was an era in which I came to terms with who I am and the way I wanted to live my life. In the '60s, I was part of the generation that turned on, tuned in, and dropped out. In the '70s, along with a multitude of others, I took a stand and declared myself to the world. Since then, the world has changed in many dramatic ways. Some of those changes have benefited gay people, women, and people of color. As a gay woman of color, I know that the change is real. But how much the world has changed, or whether it has changed at all, is critically dependent on one's nationality, economic status, religious background and affiliation, and on where one lives and travels.

I have lived openly as a gay woman for nearly four decades. Being open didn't happen overnight—in those first years of emerging from the closet, coming out was a gradual affair. But even now, when my same-sex partnership is pretty much a given wherever I am and wherever I go, I take care about where I live and travel.

I choose to live where liberals and progressives form a major part of the community, and where most people are educated and open-minded. I'm fortunate, in that I have the means to make that choice. I'm also fortunate to have been born into a time when gay people fought for recognition. We won both recognition and acceptance on a scale I could barely have dreamed of when I first realized I was gay.

That increased acceptance is true in a general way, and in a very personal way: my friend Patience, who was so uncomfortable when I came out to her in 1973—who told me she had always been made to think of homosexuality as a "distortion"—has come to a new understanding and acceptance of gay people. I believe that change in her is due in some measure to my being open with her, in the same way that others changed their view of homosexuals when we were no longer the unknown and faceless—when we became, instead, a friend, a neighbor, a family member—people they know, like, love. Patience and I have remained friends, and she welcomed my life partner into her circle when I first introduced her. She made it a point to get to know her and always extends to her the genuine warmth and affection she showers on her friends and loved ones.

Though these changes in perception and attitude are welcome, they are not universal; there are certain countries where I will not travel, just as there are certain states in the U.S. where I am reluctant to go. They are the same American states, cities, and rural areas where I will not live, because, in my opinion, life for a gay person in those places is too difficult—and sometimes downright dangerous.

These are all decisions and choices I must consider because of whom I love. In this twenty-first century world, there are still religious groups who condemn me—sight unseen—for being gay. The most extreme among them rank my sexuality as a perversion. I'm always stunned when I see or hear the contempt these zealots spew at gay people.

Their view of me bears no resemblance to the reality of who I am or the way I live my life. It is both sad and disturbing to see how their perspective and their opinions have been distorted by the fire and brimstone preaching handed down decade after decade through the centuries. In our present-day world, a few of these preachers may have modified their tone, but their sermonizing still condemns gay people to hell. And no matter what I think, whether I respond to their condemnation or let it be, their judgments are still passed on to those who are vulnerable to their extreme views. The zealots continue to breed hatred and intolerance.

Around the edges of that hard core extremism are those who call homosexuality a lifestyle, insisting that it's a choice, a preference for one kind of life over another. Where to start? To say that a person has a gay lifestyle is to reduce the complex inner life of that person to a set of likes and dislikes. You can choose, adopt or cultivate a lifestyle. You may prefer the slow pace of a small town to the high energy of a large metropolis. You may adopt a Zen simplicity in your surroundings, or prefer an array of eclectic objects in every room. You may choose to travel by bicycle rather than own a car. These are choices that reveal one's lifestyle.

There is no choice in the awareness that I am attracted to someone, or drawn to them. There is no preference involved in the feeling that I'm in love. I may prefer not to be in love with a certain person. I may prefer that they return the feeling. But the feeling itself does not arise from a conscious choice. Being attracted to someone, loving them, is visceral, instinctual, sexual, emotional. These urges and feelings are about substance rather than style. Love and sex are basic and primal. They are about life, not lifestyle.

When I realized I was gay, I wasn't able to ponder the essential question in Hamlet's soliloquy— "To be or not to be"—except in the sense that I had to ask myself whether I wanted to be fully alive, or settle for something less. When I discovered I was attracted to women, I had a choice to accept the reality of my feelings or deny them—to live a lie, or be true to myself. My choice was either to subvert my feelings and behave as society expected me to or to acknowledge my feelings and simply be myself.

These were critical life decisions. They can only be considered preferences in the sense that I preferred not to lead a covert emotional life, or a deceptive social life. I chose honesty. I preferred peace of mind.

Being gay is who I am, akin to my skin color, blood type, and the color of my eyes. No amount of analysis, programming, or impassioned persuasion to live my life differently is going to change the fact of my sexuality. No political or religious organization, no group of people, no matter how vociferous or adamant, can cause me to stop loving the person I love. No nation or government, no statute or law, can cause me to change who I am. Because being gay isn't a choice. I saw a Pride slogan recently that says it succinctly: "I was born this way."

In countries where homosexuality is equated with criminal behavior, the laws succeed only in driving people underground. Men and women who love someone of their own gender must keep their real lives hidden: that's their reality, the bitter pill they swallow each day in order to stay out of prison and stay alive. It doesn't change the essence of who they are; it only drives what is essential and real in them—their capacity to love—into the shadows.

Religions that condemn gay people drive some of their flock away. To my mind, those who are sent into exile are the fortunate ones. Losing one's religion may not seem like good fortune to those who experience it. But that loss may at least give those individuals a chance to affirm who they are. The less fortunate are those who remain closeted in order to keep their religion: some of them twist their emotions into self-hatred and hostility toward others, some live half-lives, never fully realizing a sense of complete self-expression or wholeness. And some cannot bear the struggle, the pain of living an internal exile. For them, the struggle too often ends in the tragedy of suicide.

Here in America, where gay people are afforded what amounts to second-class citizenship, the fight to claim full citizenship continues. I've never considered myself an activist, though I have joined certain movements that could not have happened without activists to lead the way. I marched to protest the war in Vietnam and the war in Iraq. I marched in the first Gay Pride Parade in San Francisco. When there are candidates and causes I believe in and care about, I've volunteered time and money. I feel a certain indebtedness to those who dedicate their lives to the political sphere and who, through their efforts in that arena, have helped bring about some of the changes that have made my life better.

I belong in a different arena. My role as an artist is to examine life and the world—to reflect the world as I see and imagine it, as I experience and envision it. Had I buckled to the forces bent on locking me away from love, I never could have seen life clearly nor imagined it fully. Had I acquiesced to the voices insisting that my search for love could be directed only toward the opposite sex, I could never have realized the whole of who I am. I could not have been myself.

The turning point in the last century, when gay people stood up for their right to live and love in the open, brought an enormous benefit to the society as a whole. It meant that all of us who had come out could give ourselves fully to our own life path, whatever that path might be. And in my worldview, each person who is able to live honestly increases the possibility of good for everyone.

Yet even as I write this, there are countless numbers of gay people who spend their days and nights thinking and feeling that there is something wrong with them, that an essential part of who they are must be changed, must be fixed. At the same time, there are far too many heterosexuals who spend some portion of their lives in the same way, thinking that every homosexual must be changed, must be fixed. Most of those who want to fix gay people are "religious." Most of them are straight, while some are in denial and only insist that they're straight. Many of these self-proclaimed righteous individuals believe that gay people, whether known to them or not, must be "saved" from the sin of homosexuality.

Those who cannot accept gay people for who they are seem to spend a great deal of their time on a non-existent problem, while gay people who cannot accept themselves expend their energy in the agony of denial and self-condemnation. All this, when there are so many real problems to address. For the individual who is gay, it can mean a life never fully lived. For the general population, it is a terrible waste of time, energy, and resources. It is regression.

Since the mid-twentieth century, we have been able to see, in the larger society, what is possible when this burden of judgment is lifted from individuals. The revolution of the '60s turned the wheel for many people, and it has had a profound and lasting effect. There are personal stories of happiness in experiencing one's own worth, in being able to live honestly and love openly. Accomplished gay people are now visible in every field of endeavor; they are addressing real problems, and contributing to the larger good.

A decided part of that good has been an infusion of new energy into the economy. Venues that existed in a closeted world can now thrive and prosper. New venues have been established and a whole range of services and products for gay people has expanded the cycle of supply and demand. When we decided to be ourselves, to live full and open lives, we also became something that entrepreneurs and business people of all stripes covet—an emerging market. That market "niche" has continued to grow, and it is now a permanent feature of the economic landscape. When we came out of the closet, we became, in one fell stroke, a political, cultural and economic force.

To the degree that gay people have found acceptance within themselves and in American society, we are made a better society and a better nation. I hope for a day when acceptance is so fully integrated that it is the norm and unremarkable. I believe each step along the path toward that day leads us ever closer to the true meaning of our Declaration of Independence.

That Declaration states that we are all created equal. As Americans, we proudly claim that we are endowed "... with certain inalienable Rights, that among these are Life, Liberty and the pursuit of Happiness." One profoundly important aspect of that pursuit lies in our search for love. Reflecting on my past and on my evolution has highlighted for me a core belief about equality: for the citizens of these United States who are gay, real equality is not possible so long as committed love is defined only as the love between a man and a woman. In that narrow definition of love, union and marriage, we exclude those who find their true nature, and find the meaning of love, in someone of their own gender. In excluding them, we circumscribe their civil and human rights.

Whom we love is central to who we are, because love itself is at the core of our existence. All of us need water, light, and food to exist. In order to survive, we need shelter from extremes of cold and heat. And to be fully alive, we need love. It is the source, the emotional engine that drives us to realize our full potential. Whomever and whatever we love—a person, a family, a place, work that we love, an idea we love, love of country—in all these expressions of commitment to what we value, it is love that is the invisible and enduring force. It is love that enables us to deal with the mundane and small necessities of day-to-day life, and it is love that inspires us to reach for the impossible and improbable dream.

Each of us is endowed with the inalienable right to claim our full measure of life, liberty, and the pursuit of happiness. In order to claim that full measure, we must be true to ourselves. An essential part of living that truth lies in acknowledging the people we love. The right to acknowledge those whom we love—and to state our commitment to them—is an integral part of the self-evident truths that form the foundation of our freedom.

December 2010. Monday evening. It's been raining all day long. A constant wind is blowing, bending the trees toward the east. I keep still, and listen to the wind chimes at the front door sending their silver music into the night. At times, the rain spatters hard against the windows, and I'm grateful to be indoors, safe and warm.

Since the autumn day when I first wrote this chapter, the world has changed again. A week ago, President Obama signed into law the repeal of Don't Ask, Don't Tell. His signature on that piece of paper means that gay people serving in the military will no longer be required to hide their sexual identity. Those joining up do not have to fear expulsion because of whom they love. Those who were discharged because of this policy have the option to return to the military. This is my journal entry written on the day that Don't Ask was repealed:

"All this morning and early afternoon I felt good. Light. Happy. I went for a long walk at mid-day. It was cold, but there was a little sun break. I came back to the house and worked for a while in the garden. Couldn't name a reason for the lightness in me. I had slept well, but it was more than that. I felt as if something had changed in the universe. Or maybe something had changed in my universe. It turned out to be both."

That afternoon, December 18, I was on the Internet and—minutes after the event—I got an email from Organizing for America. It was a message from the President, stating that the Senate had repealed Don't Ask, Don't Tell, and confirming he would sign it into law the following week.

There it was. The change in the universe. The change in my universe. The inexplicable lightness of being is this: Go ahead and ask. I can tell.

Martin Luther King told us that "... the arc of the moral universe is long, but it bends toward justice." I feel as if I traveled the arc of the moral universe in the joy I experienced on that December day. I saw the arc in the celestial spectacle of a full lunar eclipse two days later. I felt it in the conjunction of the eclipse with solstice, the first such conjunction in four hundred and fifty-six years. What does it mean? I don't know. It seemed, to me, a benediction.

There is still a distance to travel. We have further to go. We can, and we will, continue. Only now, we can breathe easier along the way, for the arc has brought us closer to the promise of our democracy.

THE LOVE OF MY LIFE

In the summer of 1978, on a day soon after I first arrived in Los Angeles, I left my apartment late in the afternoon and drove until I reached Westwood, the neighborhood that is home to UCLA. I followed the directions I had been given until I found a wide, quiet street called Beverly Glen Boulevard. The sun had just begun its slow descent toward the ocean. It was that magic hour I loved in LA, when the city was bathed in a golden-rose light.

I was on my way to spend an evening with someone I hadn't seen or spoken to in over a decade. I first met Donna in New York in 1963. At the time of our meeting, I remember thinking she was one of the kindest and most intelligent women I had ever known or could hope to know. For one summer in Manhattan, we lived in the same building and frequented the same circles. We had between us a scattering of shared social experiences, a number of wonderful conversations, and a few friends in common. Both of us had a love of theatre, film, and books. And we both, at separate times, had been in love with the same woman.

As my car rolled down the street, I saw Donna standing in front of her place on Beverly Glen. She was tall and slender, with dark hair curling into gray, and so beautiful in the twilight air that, for a moment, I was breathless. It would take months to renew our friendship, months to court and win her, but something in me knew, that evening when I first saw her again, that I had come to my deep-down bedrock place. My search was over, and I came to rest. I had found her.

CAROLYN, STEPHANIE, SARA

Carolyn, the Nordic beauty and shy romantic who first struck me as someone who had stepped out of the eighteenth century, never found her place in the modern world. Her intense mood swings plagued her; they required an ever-increasing amount of psychic energy, and they eroded her claim to some measure of emotional stability. That interior roller coaster, along with her nearly constant search to earn a living as a creative artist, meant an ongoing struggle to attain any meaningful share of financial security. But she kept at it, continuing to come back from depressed states, even though her life became more and more jumbled.

Before moving to Los Angeles in 1978, I stopped by a school out in the Fillmore District of San Francisco. Carolyn had a part-time, temporary position there as part of an arts program. It was a Saturday afternoon, and she wanted to show me the puppets she was making. It was work she loved doing. She simply wanted to do more of it and to earn a living wage for the work. Like many artists I knew, Carolyn had endured a hand-to-mouth existence for a long time. She hoped—as I did—that this arts program position marked a turning point. We visited for a while in a big classroom with high windows looking out on maple trees and a blue sky, just the two of us and an array of puppets, each of them on their way to becoming somebody.

Soon afterwards, I moved south and lost touch with her. I didn't know that the wolf that had been circling at Carolyn's door had finally walked in and taken up residence. Carolyn decided to leave it all to the wolf. One sunlit day in the spring of 1981, she walked alone onto the Golden Gate Bridge. She stood at the railing, looked out to the sea, then lay her backpack down and, along with it, her burden of cares. She plummeted into the Pacific.

A great circle of women gathered to remember her. For a period of time, I had been in love with Carolyn. All of us there had befriended her, cared for her. Yet, in her effort to make peace with herself, none of us seemed able to ease her path; none of us were able to point a way toward resolution. None of us knew how to help her turn away from the relentless despair that dominated her life. We didn't know how to keep her with us. We lost her.

Stephanie and I became lovers in the fall of 1972. Early in the new year, we began living together. In the span of a year and a half, for various reasons, we lived in three different places. Late in the spring of 1974, we started our experiment of living apart while continuing to be lovers; we also agreed on the freedom to see other people. What we discovered was that neither of us seemed able or willing to let go of our relationship.

In the summer of 1975, we decided to try setting up house again. We found a ground-floor basement apartment in Berkeley with a huge backyard that was enclosed by tall bamboo. We had limited means and two dogs, so the grand exterior compensated for the dreary interior. Our landlady paid for insulation material and Stephanie put a lot of time, energy, and labor into installing it. We both did our best to lend warmth and cheer to the apartment with our personal belongings. But the place was ill-fated. No matter what we did or how we tried, it was still a basement—damp, cold, dark. We managed to make it through the fall and winter. Then, in the spring of 1976, we gave up the ghost and split up for good.

Stephanie and I couldn't make it work, but it had still added up to four good years. Though we ended our union, our friendship continued. She remained one of my closest friends until the end, which came too soon. Stephanie died young.

There were so many of us who loved her, and it hurt terribly to lose her. We count ourselves lucky to have known her, and fortunate, in that she made one recording of her original songs. For those of us who made music with her, for everyone who heard her sing and play her guitar and her fiddle, her music remains. She was funny, generous, talented. We remember her when we eat well and drink fine wine, and when we have an excellent cup of coffee. We remember her in good music, in laughter, in the warmth of friendship. The world is poorer without her, and those who knew her are enriched always by her memory.

Sara and I never saw each other again. The last time I checked, in a remote Internet way, she was still alive and well and doing the work she wanted to do. I have one photograph of her, which I love. Her head is bent, her thick, dark hair cascades around her face; a luminous spirit is in her eyes. For me, she will always be the most blessed of beings, because she is herself, Sara.

A WEAVE OF WOMEN

November 2011. Wednesday. I take a late afternoon walk to catch the last hour of daylight on this cloudy, cold day. In every direction, wherever I look, the trees are in full autumn regalia. Fall color is everywhere—in the trees, the shrubs, the leaves strewn on the sidewalks and lawns. My world is drenched in beauty.

I take a familiar route, heading east toward a neighborhood park. On each side of the boulevard there is a long row of tall maples that sweep me up in their autumnal majesty. As I round the curve, the maples come to an abrupt end, and I look ahead to a flat stretch that is nearly devoid of trees. I cross the boulevard and turn at the first street, leaving the main thoroughfare to walk in an area of modest, well-tended houses.

One block in, I come to a house on the corner with an ample yard open to the sidewalk. In October and November, I always want to cross the yard to the apple tree behind the house. It is the same tree, with its bounty unharvested, that I've seen each year since moving to this neighborhood. The grass around the sturdy trunk is scattered with ripe fruit sinking into the earth. Each fall season, I've taken note of the fruit that has fallen to the ground, to lay there, forgotten. I have sometimes imagined myself stopping to ask the people who own this place if I can help them harvest their apples. Each year, I go by their house. Each year, I let it be. I've never had the courage to knock on their door.

I walk on, toward a row of evergreens and thick juniper bushes. I slow my pace as I pass them, lingering to breathe in the sharp scent of pine. In the distance, I see a thin curl of smoke from someone's chimney and then, as I round another corner, there is the distinct smell of fresh apples. I think they must be cut open, perhaps peeled and filling up a bowl. I imagine them on a table next to a kitchen window, ready to be made into a pie. I take it all in, reaping the color, the smells, the feel of autumn and the approach of winter.

I began this memoir in the fall, two years ago. It seems fitting that I bring it to a close in the same season. My mood when I began these pages was one of melancholy. What I feel now is gratitude. I'm grateful for my life, for my good health and for my senses that can experience the changing seasons. I'm grateful that I'm still strong, that I'm able to take a long walk on a cold day. Grateful to return, at the end of my walk, to someone I love, to a house that is peaceful and welcoming.

The someone who welcomes me home is Donna, the love of my life. Our story began in Manhattan, in 1963.

The previous year, I had begun a relationship with Aurelia; it was my first relationship with a woman. When Aurelia moved from San Francisco to New York to pursue a profession in theatre, I traveled east to spend the summer with her. Donna lived on the ground floor of the building where Aurelia had a fifth-floor walk-up.

I liked Donna and found her easy to talk with—her perspective on issues was often starkly different from the viewpoints expressed by others, and that quality in her intrigued me. She had an engaging mind and she was an open, kind person. In addition to various shared interests, we discovered that she and I also knew many of the same people in the San Francisco theatre community. We became friends over the course of the summer.

In August, I went back to California to complete my final year of college at San Francisco State. During that year, I proceeded to undo my relationship with Aurelia by becoming involved with Madeline. When Madeline and I left Sausalito and moved to New York two years later, I saw Donna only a few times before she moved back to the West Coast. For the next 13 years, we had no contact at all.

I was thirty-six when our paths intersected for a third time in Los Angeles. By then, I had been involved with several people, both women and men, though my true relationships had always been with women. Over the years, I had lived with five different women; I had never lived with a man.

I fell hard for Donna early on, but she was not easily won—it was several months before our renewed friendship became an affair—and I wasn't taking anything for granted. In case it didn't work out, I had a plan B—an exit strategy. The strategic exit was to tell myself it was all right if the relationship with Donna wasn't forever; I was glad to be with her for as long as it lasted. That was the story I told myself, and it was pure fiction. The reality was: I wanted it to last forever.

In addition to my feigned *que sera, sera* attitude, I had two other potential scenarios that might serve as ways to retreat, if needed. In one of those scenarios, I continued a long-distance relationship with David, who lived in San Francisco. David had been a college sweetheart; he had become an important friend who was an on-again, off-again lover. His world was in the sciences, mine was in the arts. Because of that difference, as well as other factors, we had seldom been favored by proximity. But David wrote me wonderful letters that ensured our connection over the years and the distances that separated us. He also had a flair for romance. During those times when we lived in the same general area—and neither of us was with someone else—he would court and win me again and we'd get back together. We had become on-again lovers shortly before I moved to Los Angeles.

The other scenario was to see if my casual relationship with a young man named Hal might become more serious. I met Hal in LA, so we were new to each other and keeping it light. We enjoyed the time we spent together, and neither of us was feeling pressed to ask for anything more.

I had been seeing both David in San Francisco and Hal in LA before Donna and I became lovers. When I look back at that time period, I can only surmise that the four of us were able to cope with our multiple *liaisons* because they were all out in the open. There were no secret assignations, no lies to tell. We were single, sexually active adults living our lives and trying out possible partnerships. But I knew this state of affairs couldn't last, nor did I want it to. Once I became involved with Donna, I felt the need to make some decisions, and soon.

When I left San Francisco to move to LA, my understanding with David was that there were no strings attached. But he was serious enough about our affair to travel to LA as often as his finances and work would allow. When Donna became part of my life, David began to ask where he and I were headed—did I see a real future for the two of us?

Any objective observer who took time to review my emotional history might have remarked that it was unlikely I was going to end up with a man, but I was hedging my bets, buffering my heart against a day when I might have to give up on being with Donna.

Although I may have imagined my alternate scenarios with David and Hal were viable, the truth was that I was spending almost all of my time with Donna. One evening, when I had been with her for a long weekend, I realized I had a cold coming on, or—worse still—the flu. Whatever it was, it was coming on fast. I suddenly felt terrible; I was feverish and weak. At that point, it had been three days and nights since I had been back to my own apartment, and my intention was to make the long drive over the hill to North Hollywood, where I lived. But instead of pulling myself together, I gave in to my misery and asked Donna if I could stay a little longer, just until I felt better.

"My darling Cristina," she said, "you can stay until you're old and gray and dead."

It was then I realized I could let go of my exit strategies. I was where I wanted to be, and I could rest in the knowledge that Donna wanted me there with her.

Not long after that evening, with both of us clear that we wanted to stay together, Donna laid down the ground rules. She stated, unequivocally, "It's you and me, kid, and nobody else—no fooling around. I'm not kidding."

I have had the profound luxury of being with her ever since, and expect to be until the day I die.

When I was growing up, I moved every year, sometimes twice in the same year. As a young adult, I kept the rhythm of an Army brat, moving often from place to place, even when I stayed in the same region for a stretch of years. That all changed when I began my love affair with Donna.

In the spring of 1979, I left my North Hollywood apartment and moved in with Donna on Beverly Glen Boulevard in West LA. She lived in a two-story, white stone building that was built into a sloping hillside.

Sex and Soul Redux

We were upstairs, in the only apartment on the second floor. It was small and lovely. Our windows looked out on trees and foliage in all directions, and they provided a graceful, leafy-green screen between us and our neighbors. A door at the back led out to a balcony, where the fragrance of clustered white privet flowers filled the air.

Now and then, in the dark, a songbird warbled outside our bedroom window. I'll never really know what kind of bird it was, but its song was so beautiful that I was convinced it must be the fabled nightingale. One night as I lay in bed, listening to that exquisite song, Donna came up from sleep and I heard her say, "Oh sweet purple cry." The poet, speaking from her bed of dreams, capturing the essence of the nightingale's song in four words.

We were there at Beverly Glen for nearly six years, longer than I had ever lived anywhere in my entire life.

We moved to San Francisco in December 1984. Stephanie and her lover, Nora, drove down to LA in Stephanie's van to help us with the move. Stephanie took all our plants and furniture in the van; Donna and I packed our clothes and smaller items into our separate cars. Donna took our cat, Rom, with her; I took our dog Tofu. Before leaving, Donna went on at length about a temporary confinement of our cat: once we were in San Francisco, Rom was not to go outside for at least three days. We must absolutely keep him in until he knew where home was—she didn't want him to get lost in the new neighborhood. When I arrived at 4th Avenue that evening, Donna was already there, as were my mother and Chet, the man in her life. Rom was nowhere to be seen. It turned out that one of the first things Donna had done was to let him go outside to the fenced-in back yard.

"Why?" I asked.

Her answer: "He wanted to go out."

Ever the king in our household, Rom got his way. No matter, he knew where home was. He had two women who loved him and a dog who doted on him. And, with us, he always ate well.

We had given my mother the key to the house and, when we all finally arrived (Stephanie had taken an inadvertent detour and nearly ended up in Fresno), she had the house warmed up and food—both immediate snacks and a full meal— prepared for the weary travelers. My mother and stepfather had finalized their divorce more than a decade earlier. After she had recovered from the trauma and near breakdown the divorce had caused her, my mother found Chet, a big bear of a man who was loving and funny and strong. Chet helped us unload everything. When we sat down to the delicious food my mother had made, she presented Donna and me with our first housewarming gift: a large round cutting board with grooved edges. We still have it; we still use it.

A few weeks later, when we had begun to claim our new house and make it our home, my mother showed up with another gift—my hope chest. It was, and is, a handsome and substantial piece of furniture, a teak chest with brass fittings—its sides and lid beautifully carved with scenes from ancient China. At my mother's request, my stepfather had bought it in Hong Kong many years before, when I was still a teenager. It is, I think, an indication of the wedding my mother had been hoping for when it was purchased; she wanted me to marry well. In February 1985, when she brought it to us, Donna and I had just celebrated our sixth anniversary. As we placed the chest in an alcove of our living room, I knew that, in my mother's mind, I had settled down for good. It wasn't a legal marriage, and there had been no wedding. But as far as Louise was concerned, in my choosing Donna, I had married well.

I had been the one to initiate the move to San Francisco. I had several reasons for wanting to leave LA. More than anything else, I wanted to be near my mother as she got older. She had done so much for me, yet whenever I asked her what I could do for her, she asked for only one thing: she wanted me to be with her, to help her, when she could no longer do for herself. The move to San Francisco gave me another fourteen years to enjoy and experience her laughter and her stories, her wonderful cooking and generosity, and her sometimes exasperating independence and stubbornness.

In February 1998, I got a call from her in the middle of the night. I had to rush to take her to the hospital—she refused to call 911—and the unraveling began. In the last year of her life, as she faded away, I was able to keep my promise to her. Donna's ever-present love and support, along with the help of a close-knit circle of friends, enabled me to stay with her so she could live, and die, in her own home. Louise left us in October 1999. I've always been glad I was near her for those final years, and with her at the end.

Though the concern for my mother may have been the driving force behind my desire to return to San Francisco, I was also keenly aware of a certain restlessness of spirit in me—an inability to settle in Southern California. I was grounded in my relationship with Donna, but I had a sense of being adrift in Los Angeles. I felt pulled to San Francisco and to the bay, with its bridges spanning the water. I missed the counties of a beautiful region that had been home for many years—Marin and Alameda, Sonoma and Napa. Along with my love for the entire area, I had a shared history with an extended family of friends there. They were part of everything that connected me to Northern California.

Donna had lived in San Francisco twice before, for a short while in the late '50s and again in the early '60s. On the last of our trips north from LA, as she tried on the idea of living in San Francisco again, Donna found that she felt at home in the cafés of the city. They suited her, and she loved the perfect cappuccinos the baristas made. At the time, smokers hadn't yet been exiled to the great outdoors, and she could smoke in restaurants and bars and cafés. That meant she could linger over a cappuccino and a cigarette, and savor it all—the scent of chocolate sprinkled over foamy milk, the flavor mixed with smoke and the dark tobacco taste of her cigarette. She told me the combination made for a deeply pleasurable experience.

While it's true that cappuccinos played an important part in our change of locale, I think our move may have been finally decided by piroshki—specifically, the piroshki in the House of Piroshki delicatessen on 9th Avenue. The taste of the warm, golden-brown dough with its savory filling convinced Donna she would be all right with packing up our household and heading north.

The House of Piroshki is gone now, but at the time it was owned by an old Russian who stationed himself out front to greet and help customers. He employed a team of women in a large unadorned kitchen at the back of the deli. I remember glancing into the kitchen one day to see the women in plain white aprons, talking and laughing as they worked. They made food that I still sometimes crave.

We stayed in San Francisco for twenty-two years. Twelve of them were spent near Golden Gate Park on 4th Avenue, where we found a spacious first-floor flat in an old Edwardian house. It had high ceilings, a big kitchen with a real pantry, and a dining room with a built-in hutch. There was a large living room with a wonderful alcove and a bay window at the front, and a huge yard in the back. It was drafty and nearly impossible to heat in the winter, but we loved having all that room and a place that was amenable to our pets.

The bay window at the front flooded the interior with light, and provided a great showcase at Christmastime, when we would hoist a pine or spruce tree that was always at least eight feet high. We would trim it splendidly with decorations chosen from a plentiful collection, then finish it with myriad tiny white lights. It always delighted our friends and our neighbors. I remember walking along the street one evening, seeing the Christmas tree in the window and thinking to myself, what a wonderful home that must be, and being filled with happiness that it was mine.

The tenants before us had left the backyard untended; it had been overtaken by weeds—most of them knee-high and deep-rooted. Our hard labor and determination transformed the dirt, broken stone and weeds into a garden. We put in a lush strip of lawn for our dog Tofu to roll around on, and my mother gave me jade plants, cymbidium orchids, spearmint, and white alyssum from her garden. I planted tea tree bushes with miniature, deep-pink flowers, and I scattered California poppy seeds everywhere. The poppies thrived and when spring came, we were treated to a riot of golden-orange color.

There was a graceful bamboo that served as a focal point at the far end of the yard, and a wood bench to one side of the garden, where we could sit and contemplate our bit of paradise. It was all enclosed by a high wooden fence that our cat strode on like a king surveying his realm. Our second summer there, we discovered that the slender trees all around the edge of the garden were

Italian plums, and each year, they rewarded our labor with delicious fruit.

When the house was sold in 1996, we had to find new digs. Since old age had taken both our cat and dog from us, we decided not to try to replicate what we had on 4th Avenue. We moved to the outskirts of the city, to a much smaller space that will remain in my memory as a grand apartment.

It was at the top of a twelve-story building. It had beautiful hardwood floors, a walk-in closet off the master bedroom, and big windows that looked out over parkland, Lake Merced, and the Pacific Ocean. My mother always called it the penthouse. We were there for ten years before we made the decision to bid farewell to our life in San Francisco.

Now we live in a small Northwestern university town. The move here was initiated by Donna. She had been working full-tilt her entire life, and as she got older and took on more responsibility, she began averaging a sixty-hour work week on a regular basis. She kidded about dying at her desk, but as her workload increased, it became less a joke and more a distinct possibility. When she received the completely unexpected news that a younger friend of hers who lived in Los Angeles had died, it seemed to bring home the message that we never know how much time we have. A voice inside told her to stop and smell the roses now, because tomorrow might be too late.

Donna's idea of stopping to smell the roses was a life in which the two of us had the freedom to do as we liked with our time. That meant we would both stop working. She had watched me over the years fit my creative work into evenings and weekends—it was the trade-off I had made while keeping a day job—jobs that supported my writing habit and enabled me to contribute my share to a fairly secure and comfortable life with Donna.

Early on in our years together, I taught Tai Chi at various nonprofit organizations and community centers in the greater Los Angeles area. While it was satisfying work, the financial rewards were less than sufficient. This way of earning my living required a lot of travel and an entrepreneurial zeal that I lacked. I gave up my freeform work life and secured a position as an administrative assistant to a professor at the Geophysics Institute at UCLA, where I earned a steady paycheck with benefits and met a lot of interesting scientists. Some of the young men among them would later be known as geeks. From them, I learned a new form of typing called word processing.

After two years at UCLA, I found the same sort of work at a large nonprofit organization. When we moved to San Francisco, there was a brief period when I worked as a freelance illustrator; apart from that time, I continued to earn my income at nonprofits, progressing from administrative assistant to office manager.

I never quite got the concept of retiring, because I always saw myself as a writer and an artist, and it seemed to me that you kept on writing and making art until you dropped dead. When Donna began to broach the subject of retiring, she would ask the same question in various ways. The question was: "Wouldn't you like to wake up in the morning and write?" The idea of spending my time doing what I loved to do, rather than what I had to do to earn a paycheck, certainly had appeal. Only I wasn't sure how we could manage it. Donna made some calculations. She determined we could manage it by finding a place to live where a reduced income would still allow us to enjoy what we value in life.

We traveled to Oregon to visit a friend in Corvallis in May 2006. There were tree-lined streets and gardens everywhere, and all of it in bloom. The days were sunlit and warm. I was charmed by the downtown area of cafés and restaurants, bookstores and small shops. I imagined myself spending hours in the reading room of the library, where I could settle into an armchair and look out through the high arched windows to the city's Central Park. The presence of the university made for a well-educated and diverse community that valued the arts, sciences and the humanities. Though I loved big city life, I had sometimes entertained a fantasy of living in a small American town. Corvallis seemed to be the ideal flowering of that fantasy.

When asked what she does here, Donna is fond of saying she leads the life of Picasso. "Not that I make art like Picasso," she adds. "Only that, like him, I arise in the early afternoon and then do as I please."

As for me, I have come into a time best described by a man named Ernest Benn, who said, "Liberty is being free of the things we don't like, in order to be slaves of the things we do like." I am now at liberty to be enslaved by art. I am free to be a writer, free to make art, free to dance to my heart's content. The other morning in dance class, I looked in the mirror and realized I was wearing slacks, shirt, and shoes befitting Gene Kelly in *Singin' in the Rain*. I remembered wanting to be Gene Kelly, and I remembered my mother, who first taught me to dance. Look, Ma, I thought. I'm dancing.

Late November, 2011. Dawn. Monday. The fog that came in the night is slowly lifting. I hear a train rumbling by in the distance, its low horn sounding out three warnings of its approach. I go to my desk, settle in, and look up from a narrow-lined yellow pad to a black-and-white photograph propped against a jar of pens. The photo is of my grandmother and me in front of her house in the Philippines. I was about six years old when it was taken. Romana is in her fifties.

There is a sense of play about her—you can see it in her smile and the tilt of her chin. And along with that playfulness you can see in her firm stance that she can be counted on, and that you'd better not tangle with her or anyone in her care.

Romana was tiny—when I was only six years old, the top of my head was already at her shoulder. Yet in

Sex and Soul Redux

her small frame resided all the strength and competence I knew so well in my mother.

On the bookcase across from my desk is a photo of my mother when she was in her mid-thirties. I think of the sacrifices she made when I was a baby, keeping me safe and fed during the harsh conditions of war and our imprisonment in a Japanese prison camp. I remember, when I was twelve, she was suddenly there to rescue me from a fierce dog who had gone into attack mode and was about to go for my throat. My mother beat him away with a broom and a ferocity he couldn't match. More than once she shielded me from danger; more often than I can count, she nursed me back from illness and injury.

After my mother died, at age 87, I was looking at this photo and saw that the brim of her hat forms a halo, and the foliage behind her appears to give her wings. She was my angel.

I turn toward a mahogany cabinet behind me and consider a photo of Donna that I took thirty years ago, when we were in Maui to mark my fortieth birthday. We were at a hillside restaurant called Pineapple Hill in Kapalua. Donna is on the terrace, looking out to the ocean, serene and beautiful. I see in her smile her delight in the moment, her love of life. Each day with her, in her appreciation for both ordinary and extraordinary things—the way she savors a good cup of tea, or is thrilled by a spectacular sunset—I appreciate that love anew.

Romana, the woman who gave my mother life, Louise, the woman who gave me life, and Donna, with whom I have made a life—these three women are at the core of my being. They form the central threads in the weave of women who have been my salvation.

Wednesday. The last day of November. I stand outside the front door for a while, eyes closed, face turned up to the warmth of a mid-day sun. I hear a rustling sound and open my eyes to see yellow-gold leaves being carried away by a gust of wind. The leaves have been torn from the three tall poplar trees at the edge of the driveway. The poplars are magnificent; their nearly barren branches seem to brush the sky. I always think of them as watching over us.

I believe I have become more a pantheist than a Christian—or perhaps that was always my bent, even as a child. In the eclectic mix that has become my religion, in moments like this—when I am truly present and aware—I understand that all things are holy.

I watch the poplar leaves drift across a patch of brilliant blue sky. In the distance, thick clouds gather to bring us more rain. I go back inside to the quiet of the house. This ground floor apartment with a small garden of flowers and herbs that I tend has been home to Donna and me since 2006. I don't know how long we'll be here, or how long we'll be in the next place—if there is another place in our future. Home is where Donna is. Our life together is where I have taken root.

Donna and I were first legally registered as domestic partners in San Francisco in 1998; we applied for and received our official certificate on our nineteenth anniversary. Eight years later, we began the move to Oregon. About eighteen months after we had settled here, a statute recognizing domestic partnerships took effect. In 2008, we celebrated our twenty-ninth anniversary by being one of the first couples in Corvallis to register as domestic partners at the Benton County Courthouse.

In our first years together, I felt some frustration at the inadequacy of language. It seemed so prosaic to introduce my soul mate as my partner. For a while, some people referred to the person they were with as their "significant other." That term seemed particularly cumbersome. The words lover, friend, companion, and helpmate were similarly inadequate. Donna is all of these to me, but none of those terms encompasses the whole of what we mean to each other. I've adapted to—and come to accept—the term "partner." In everything we do, strive for, deal with and celebrate, we are partnered. Until someone comes up with a better word, partner serves the purpose.

As for a marriage ceremony, the closest we have come was in the year 2000 when—along with many other gay couples—we took part in a Commitment Ceremony held at the resplendent San Francisco City Hall. The event was presided over by the Honorable Willie L. Brown, Jr., Mayor of San Francisco, and it was a happy occasion. Stating our commitment to one another before a city supervisor had the look and feel of a marriage ritual, but gave us no legal status. Legality and ritual aside, it is the reality of the life Donna and I have shared for over three decades that is, to my mind and heart, the equivalent of being married.

We were both well out of the closet when we fell in love, but neither of us thought we would live to see a world where marriage would one day be an option for same-sex couples. As certain states began to legalize same-sex marriage, Donna and I would often comment on—and marvel at—the progress being made. Though she applauded the new legislation, she would also point out that those marriages had limited rights and benefits: until the federal government recognizes same-sex marriage, gay married couples have no right to any of the federal benefits accorded to "traditional" marriages between men and women.

To me, the clearest example of this is that social security benefits are transferred to widows and widowers upon the death of their spouse—unless the widow was married to a woman, or the widower was married to a man. When it comes to gay couples, a valid, state-issued marriage license counts for nothing in our nation's capital.

We are awaiting the day when a same-sex marriage sanctioned by a state also qualifies as a legitimate marriage under federal law. Like all other citizens of these United States, we want all our rights, and full equality.

Donna and I have pooled our resources and money from the beginning. We've shared the sum total of physical, emotional, and financial hills and valleys of our life together. We both take on the sacrifices entailed when one of us is ill or dealing with a traumatic situation, or when friends and family are in need. Yet the federal government that annually collects taxes from both of us, considers each of us a solo act. And when death comes, as it inevitably will, the one who is left behind will be viewed—legally—as someone who has been alone for the last several decades. Neither of us will be accorded the rights and benefits our partnership warrants. If ever this inequity is resolved, Donna and I will marry.

Meanwhile, when you read this, take it as a given that I still live with, and cherish, the love of my life. Along with our shared sense of humor, her skepticism, and my faith, our love endures.

SURPRISE

I brought this memoir to a close in the fall of 2011. I then went on to the editing, revising and rewriting that are part of the territory for every writer. Meanwhile, life went on, bringing innumerable changes abroad and at home. Here in America, one change in particular was profoundly important to all of us who are gay. On the day it happened, I realized my work was not finished; another chapter had unfolded.

Summer 2013. On Wednesday morning, June 26, Donna and I were waking up in the home of our friends Cece and Anne, who live in the city of Sonoma in California. It was the day we were to begin our drive back to Oregon, after nearly two weeks of visiting friends and favorite places throughout the San Francisco Bay Area.

We were all up early. Donna and I had to get on the road; Cece and Anne had to get to work. But our shared sense of anticipation had nothing to do with travel or the workday. There was a buzz in the air because it was the morning the Supreme Court was scheduled to announce its rulings on two cases: the Defense of Marriage Act (DOMA)—the 1996 law that blocked federal recognition of gay marriage—and California's Proposition 8, which banned gay marriage in 2008. The television was on, with Rachel Maddow anchoring the coverage on MSNBC. A little after 7:00 a.m., it was announced that DOMA had been struck down. I was one of four people in that Sonoma home and one of millions around the nation who sent up a loud and joyous cheer.

But along with that cheer, in those first few seconds after hearing the ruling of the court, my response was one of stunned disbelief. Had this really happened? The federal government would now recognize the legality of same-sex marriages endorsed by individual states? Same-sex marriages would be accorded the same legal benefits as opposite-sex marriages? I honestly didn't believe it would happen in my lifetime.

Soon after that decision was announced, the Supreme Court dismissed the Prop 8 case on procedural grounds, meaning a lower-court decision that had struck down Prop 8 was left in place. There was more cheering. Cece and Anne, who have been together for twenty-five years, were married in California five years ago. The Supreme Court decision meant their marriage was now, once again, legal.

We had scheduled our California trip to suit our own timetable, and arranged our various visits to dovetail with the time that our friends had available. It had made sense to visit Cece and Anne last, as we were heading north and—of all the friends we were visiting—they live at the northernmost point. But being there with them for this momentous occasion filled me with wonder: given what seems to be the random nature of most events in our lives, we might have been anywhere on that particular morning. Instead, we were with close friends—two gay women for whom this moment in time had deep significance, just as it did for Donna and me. Sharing this event with another gay couple connected me even more vividly to all the gay couples I know and love, and it made me think of all the same-sex couples I don't know who are in committed relationships. They too, I was certain, were celebrating this event; I felt we were all joined in happiness.

Now that the elation I experienced on that landmark day is in the past, I am dealing with a new reality. Long before DOMA was struck down, Donna and I had agreed we would marry if and when the federal government legalized same-sex unions. I thought it likely that Oregon would soon recognize same-sex marriage; all the trends were pointing in that direction. But without the same rights granted by the federal government to "traditional" marriages, being married in Oregon wouldn't have the legal standing that a marriage contract is meant to provide.

My country surprised me. The "soon" I was anticipating came from the federal government, rather than from Oregon. Yes, Donna and I would like to marry.

But we currently reside in a state where a constitutional amendment excludes us from marriage. In fact, it prohibits us from attaining any form of legal family status. Oh, the irony.

We could easily travel to California, or travel an even shorter distance to Washington; neither of these states impose a residency requirement on couples wishing to marry. But traveling to a different state in order to marry, then returning home to a state where that marriage is not recognized, could put us through several legal twists and turns. In 36 other states, gay couples who want to marry are facing similar legal complications and conservative opposition.

For straight Americans who think they might one day marry, how sweet it must be not to have to face these hurdles. They have the freedom to marry the person they love; that basic right is theirs at birth. While they may have a lot to consider in contemplating marriage, having the right itself is not one of them.

As of this writing, we have not decided where or when we will marry. I can only report that Donna has proposed, and I have said yes. This was months ago, when the Supreme Court first heard the DOMA case.

"If this goes the way I think it will," Donna said, "we may have to marry."

"Yes," I said.

Beat. Beat. "You realize I'm proposing?"

"Yes! I'm thrilled." Oddly enough, it *was* thrilling, even after all these years together. "And yes, I will marry you." Beat. Beat. "It's because you want all my money, right?"

"Right."

It's an old joke between us. All my money *is* her money, and all her money is mine. It's been that way with us from the get-go. Our sense of equally shared income is another way that we're already married, even though the marriage is neither state-nor-church–sanctioned. But now we're contemplating the actuality of a state-issued marriage license, a legal document that neither of us thought we would ever be able to obtain.

We don't yet know when we will marry. It may be soon, in a border state. If Oregon voters overturn the current ban, we will marry next year, in our own state. We only know we're going forward—we will marry. The fact that we can plan to marry still amazes me.

I cannot predict—but I do hope—that same-sex couples who want to marry will be able to marry in Oregon in 2014. The narrow-mindedness that has resulted in laws treating gay people as outsiders and second-class citizens is making way for mainstream acceptance. In the months and years to come, I know more states will recognize same-sex unions. Will I live to see the day when they are recognized nationwide? Impossible to say. I don't know how long I'll live, or how long it will take for this to become a non-issue.

Perhaps my country will surprise me again.

PEACEFUL

May 2014. Blue sky, white clouds, sunlight. A perfect spring day. I walk a few blocks to the park in my neighborhood, and settle on a bench overlooking an expanse of grass and trees. I listen to birds singing, the rustle of leaves stirring in the breeze, and a metallic creaking sound coming from the playground in the distance. There are two children on the swings, their legs and feet pumping and pushing them toward the sky.

My thoughts drift away and then return again to a central event: A short while ago, a federal judge ruled that the same-sex marriage ban here in Oregon is unconstitutional. In 2004, there was only one state where gay and lesbian couples could legally marry: Massachusetts. Ten years have passed, and there has been slow and steady progress toward justice. As of today, Donna and I can give our union legal standing in the state where we live.

There is a rising tide of recognition that marriage is a civil right constitutionally given to all citizens. The forces opposed to marriage equality will go on trying to stem that tide—their efforts serve as a reminder that same-sex marriage is still banned in more than half the states, and that gay people are still viewed as immoral by many. The argument goes on, and the court battles will continue. Meanwhile, Donna and I will begin planning our marriage ceremony.

I cannot help but think about my mother, who wanted to see me married because she thought marriage would give me security, and hoped it would bring happiness. She felt I had found both security and happiness in my relationship with Donna. If Louise were still alive today, I know she would be glad for us.

I do not feel the incredulous joy I experienced when the Supreme Court struck down the Defense of Marriage Act. I feel peaceful, at one with the day, in harmony with everything and everyone I see and sense around me. I'm grateful to have lived long enough to see this moment in history, to be a part of it, and thankful for all those who worked to make it happen. For this hour in time, all's right with my world.

I head for home, and the woman I love.

EPILOGUE

In 2014, on a mild July day, Donna and I were married at the Benton County Courthouse in Corvallis, Oregon. Our ceremony was held outside on the lawn, under a clouded sky and a canopy of trees that have graced the courthouse grounds for decades. We were married by the Benton County Clerk, a gentleman whose warmth, ease, and good humor added to the happiness of this joyous occasion. Three of our dearest friends witnessed our union and celebrated with us.

After thirty-five years together, Donna and I were legal at last.

ACKNOWLEDGMENTS

Many people helped make this book possible. The original draft went to Gail Browne, who read it with great care and insight. She told me what she liked and didn't like; she also asked thoughtful questions. Those questions guided my rewrites. When I sent it to her again, several revisions later, she read the new version with equal care and reported back to me with the same attention to detail. Orpha Barry read a revised draft and gave me enthusiastic and critical feedback. She also asked an essential question—one that led me to dig deeper into my past—and that digging led to a better manuscript.

Thanks also to Salomon Bonilla, for his feedback about two places in the book where, as a reader, he wished to know more. The poem alluded to but not shared in the original edition is included in this redux edition. And I have expanded on the reasons that led me to recreate myself after a failed relationship when I first moved to Sonoma County.

Many thanks to my writing ally Marilyn Matevia, who—even in the midst of doctoral degree demands—took the time to read an early draft. A big thank you to Skye Atman, who challenged my first title. That challenge led me to search for a new title, and now, I have one that I love. To all of you, my wonderful friends, thank you.

I am grateful for finding Ray Rhamey, my book designer. His care, craftsmanship, creativity and innate sense of style turned text into a beautiful book, and his talent ensured that this memoir is a fine visual and textural experience. He is also a pleasure to work with. Thank you, Ray.

I am deeply indebted to Karen Asbelle, editor *par excellence*. Her skill, knowledge, and intelligence made this a far better book than the one I first handed over to her. If there are any errors that remain, they are mine. Karen not only made certain that my i's were dotted and my t's crossed, she also made sure I was clearly communicating what I had intended to say. In her own words, it was always about "... what serves the story best." Throughout this process, she served the story beautifully. The icing on that literary cake was that her feedback was invariably delivered with keen wit and wry humor. Karen, you are the best.

My heartfelt thanks go first, last, and always to Donna. She read the first draft, the last draft, and several revised chapters in-between, many times. Without her patience, intelligence, and wisdom to guide me, I'd be nowhere. Her common sense never fails to point me in the right direction, and her wonderful sense of humor keeps me laughing during the most trying of times. And whenever I'm consumed by the writing life, she's the one who makes sure that I continue to eat. Somewhere, somehow, I must have done something right—how else to account for the goodness that is Donna? Thank you, my love.

Thank You

Thank you for buying and reading *Sex and Soul Redux*. I hope reading it was a satisfying experience.

If you have a story you'd like to share about how this memoir has made a difference for you, a friend, or a family member, please email me: clw@cristinalwhite.com.

Since I am an independent publisher, the marketing staff at Letter Pen Press is yours truly, and readers like you who are willing to spread the word. If you enjoyed *Sex and Soul Redux,* please tell your friends, share your comments via social media networks, or post a review on Amazon and/or Goodreads. Even a sentence or two is appreciated.

I invite you to contact me and read more of my work at http://cristinalwhite.com.

Thanks,
Cristina

ALSO BY CRISTINA L. WHITE

"One Cup of Rice"
In the Anthology
Youth in Wartime: Recollections of World War II
Cave Art Press

"Forgiveness"
In Timberline Review Issue 11
Willamette Writers

"Becoming Art Deco"
In Occult Detective Magazine #8
Cathaven Press

The Healing Environment
(Authored as Cristina Ismael)
Celestial Arts

The Enchanted Journey
A play for children
Samuel French, Inc.

A complete listing of the author's published work to date is at: www.cristinalwhite.com

www.ingramcontent.com/pod-product-compliance
Lightning Source LLC
Chambersburg PA
CBHW030436010526
44118CB00011B/655